Clandestine Theology

Also Available from Bloomsbury

Anti-Badiou: On the Introduction of Maoism into Philosophy, *François Laruelle*
The Principles of Non-Philosophy, *François Laruelle*
The Last Humanity: A New Ecological Science, *François Laruelle (forthcoming)*

Clandestine Theology
A Non-Philosopher's Confession of Faith

François Laruelle
Translated by Andrew Sackin-Poll

BLOOMSBURY ACADEMIC
LONDON • NEW YORK • OXFORD • NEW DELHI • SYDNEY

BLOOMSBURY ACADEMIC
Bloomsbury Publishing Plc
50 Bedford Square, London, WC1B 3DP, UK
1385 Broadway, New York, NY 10018, USA

BLOOMSBURY, BLOOMSBURY ACADEMIC and the Diana
logo are trademarks of Bloomsbury Publishing Plc

First published in 2019 in France as *Théologie Clandestine pour les sans-religion: Une confession de foi du non-philosophe* by Editions Kimé

First published in Great Britain 2021

English Language translation Copyright © Andrew Sackin-Poll, 2021

Andrew Sackin-Poll has asserted his right under the Copyright, Designs and Patents Act, 1988, to be identified as Translator of this work.

For legal purposes the Acknowledgements on p. xii constitute
an extension of this copyright page.

Cover design by Charlotte Daniels
Cover images: Background © Max McKinnon / Unsplash
Crucifixion statue © Enrico Della Pietra / Alamy Stock Photo

All rights reserved. No part of this publication may be reproduced or transmitted in any form or by any means, electronic or mechanical, including photocopying, recording, or any information storage or retrieval system, without prior permission in writing from the publishers.

Bloomsbury Publishing Plc does not have any control over, or responsibility for, any third-party websites referred to or in this book. All internet addresses given in this book were correct at the time of going to press. The author and publisher regret any inconvenience caused if addresses have changed or sites have ceased to exist, but can accept no responsibility for any such changes.

A catalogue record for this book is available from the British Library.

Library of Congress Cataloging-in-Publication Data
Names: Laruelle, François, author. | Sackin-Poll, Andrew, translator.
Title: Clandestine theology : a non-philosopher's confession of faith / Francois Laruelle ; translated by Andrew Sackin-Poll.
Other titles: Théologie clandestine pour les sans-religion. English
Description: London ; New York : Bloomsbury Academic, 2020. | "First published in 2019 in France as Théologie Clandestine pour les sans-religion: Une confession de foi du non-philosophe by Editions Kimé." | Includes bibliographical references and index.
Identifiers: LCCN 2020019588 (print) | LCCN 2020019589 (ebook) | ISBN 9781350104310 (paperback) | ISBN 9781350104242 (hardback) | ISBN 9781350104235 (ebook) | ISBN 9781350104297 (epub)
Subjects: LCSH: Jesus Christ. | Christianity–Essence, genius, nature. | Bible. Epistles of Paul–Theology. | Philosophical theology. | Philosophy and religion.
Classification: LCC BT304.9 .L3713 2020 (print) | LCC BT304.9 (ebook) | DDC 230–dc23
LC record available at https://lccn.loc.gov/2020019588
LC ebook record available at https://lccn.loc.gov/2020019589

ISBN:	HB:	978-1-3501-0424-2
	PB:	978-1-3501-0431-0
	ePDF:	978-1-3501-0423-5
	eBook:	978-1-3501-0429-7

Typeset by Integra Software Services Pvt. Ltd.

To find out more about our authors and books visit www.bloomsbury.com
and sign up for our newsletters.

Contents

Foreword viii
Acknowledgements xii
Translator's note xiii
   Introduction xiii
   A clandestine theology xxi
   A real critique of theology by faith xxiii
   We are not survivors of the tomb xxix
   The Stranger-subject and the word xxxvii
   Laruelle and the future of theology: A theoretical liturgy xlii
   References 1

Introduction 1
   Clandestine theology: The impossible *homoousia* and the destruction of the trinity 1
   An axiomatic of the trinity 2

1 Faith and belief 7
   Man-in-person as universal *a priori* 7
   The generic style and its two interpretations 11
   The confession of faith and theological duplicity 17
   Faith and dualyzation of belief 19
   Faith, fidelity, and grace 23
   Belief as unilateral paradox 25

Faith as *a priori* posture 28
Profess or confess faith? 30
The identity-in-the-last-instance of faith and religion 31
The category of the non-religious Christian 33
The Name-of-Christ as first symbol 37
The work of the confession of faith 41
Faith transforms the works of the world 44
Faith testifies to a forced speech 47

2 The Gospels: Models for non-Christianity 51
A Gnostic Christ and the insurrection of faith 51
The words of Jesus on life 54
The sayings of Jesus: Theorems or axioms? 56
Life, living, surviving, and glorious experience 61
Christ according to St Paul: The Pauline reversal 65
St Paul according to Jesus: The Pauline inversion 70
The inverse of Christianity 74
Christ as immanent mediation or medium-without-mediation 76
Messianity as sub-version of Christianity 82
On the plane of salvation, we make a *tabula rasa* 88
The disciple and the apostle: A dualysis of the apostolic tradition 91
The *a priori* defence of faith by the paraclete 95

3 Surviving scripture, glorious scripture 99
Incarnation as clonage 99
Should Christianity be deconstructed? Surviving scripture, surviving writing 102
Glorious writing, risen among the signifying 105
A non-Catholic thesis for the use of the reformation 109
Fidelity as a rigorous method 113

A theorem of salvation as work 116
Two forms of atheism: Conformism and heresy 118
How the without-religion adopts religion 120
Heresy as theo-fiction and philo-fiction 122

4 Dualysis of the trinity 127
Dualysis of revelation 127
On the trinity as symptom 128
On the trinity as circumcession 132
In-the-last-paternity 136
How God becomes Son of Man 139

5 A clandestine non-religion 141
The Name-of-Man 141
Philosophical and religious paradigms 144
The two initial prejudices of all theology 146
A theory of radical evil 150
Post-ecclesial faith as last belief 153
The end of beliefs and the exit from the post-ecclesial 154
From the exit from belief to faithful access 158
Towards a clandestine theology – Thought-faith 159
A definitively non-sufficient grace: Against creation 162
The reformation as model for non-religion 163
The consummation of time 165
Retreat and grace 168
From sin to evil 174
A clandestine and messianic life 177

Notes 183
Index 186

Foreword

Clandestine Theology sets out the conditions for a systematic distinction between faith and belief. It is clandestine because it does not go through any of the usual paths, which, at one point or another, mix these two orders. It makes possible a reinterpretation of dogma as many models through which to understand religion afresh. This distinction thus leads to an inversion in interpretation: dogma no longer offers the means to interpret faith, but rather it is a particular result of what has already happened, for example, the resurrection, given without donation.

One knows that belief is a complex and variable mixture of languages, symbols, and generalizations about lived experiences that draw solidity and consistency from an authority that grants such an entanglement. Faith is, by contrast, a kind of Ockham's razor that remains partially indifferent to beliefs. It poses a certain resistance to beliefs, while at the same time offering the means to handle them. Faith is the function of the 'without-religion'.

Belief, therefore, has its origin in the world and the activity of subjects. It is normal in matters affecting relations between subjects and their tribulations. Through prayer, confession, and mass, the subject lives their belief. Faith is much more mysterious, however, since it does not have the immediate support of beliefs. Where does faith come from? How does it happen? Let us remember the imperative of Laruelle at the back of the review of *The Philosophical Decision*: 'Do not do like philosophers, invent philosophy! Change its practice!' Is not such an imperative an act of faith?

I would like to propose a general hypothesis about faith, as Laruelle understands it. In my opinion, it is not limited to any field. Faith is no more restricted to the field of religion than any other, like philosophy, art, and technology. As Laruelle's works show, one handles a discipline thanks only to its relation to another heterogeneous and 'under' or 'sub-' field, deployed in order to avoid the phenomenon of reversibility. See, for example, the fusion of philosophy and the quantum found 'underneath' the non-standard in *Non-Standard Philosophy*, the fusion of philosophy and theology in a 'sub-' theology in *Future Christ* and *Christo-Fiction*, and the fusion of philosophy and technology found in the ordinary of *Biography of the Ordinary Man*. This fusion is one of the effects of faith. The two opposing aspects of faith – that is, radical distinction and fusion – are made compatible in non-philosophy and non-standard philosophy.

We know that the Real and the world are radically separated by Laruelle. The Real = x is called the generic human, without qualities, and 'in' the world are subjects and their attributes. The distinction of human and subjects is a pledge of peace; exterminations, holocausts, genocides always suppose their indistinction: is it the human who is killed in the subject?

I suppose that the generic human, in his or her radical loneliness, does not need faith. This is shown through dualysis, whereby an ordinary term x is made to appear at the very edge of the relation, always indirect, between propositions made in the world and the Real. The rules of dualysis are explained in *Philosophy and Non-philosophy*. Faith would thus appear as the point of or necessary passage for the fragments of the dualistic world and the Real, rather than from the generic human, which is always indifferent to the world. Faith is like an inverted lightning, which is recreated once every time. The subject needs the human, but the human does not need the subject. The name of God is God, but God is not the name, as Hesychasm reminds us.

Let us take the idea of faith as Ockham's razor, not allowing itself to be led by belief. How does faith distance itself from belief? I would say through the 'non-' of non-philosophy and non-standard philosophy. Faith has distanced itself from philosophy to the extent that the sufficiency of the latter is understood in terms of belief. It must be re-interpreted through the prism of minority, not authority. Philosophy does not disappear, but it must be treated and made part of the 'theories' that resist this 'non-'. This resistance is essential to the practice of non-philosophy: the untreated theory becomes a material for the operators of non-philosophy, a deep and silent faith, hidden in the cavern. The 'non-' becomes like a more explicit and more expressive transformation of philosophy. The 'non-' is the worldly form of faith. It enables faith to be with the subject in all his or her mutations and stases.

It should be noted that this 'non-' does not relate to a verb but to a noun – 'philosophy' – and makes an extension of it possible. Non-philosophy is precisely not the end of philosophy. The 'non-' then relates to an adjective: the non-standard. Between the two, there is a softening in the non-standard, philosophy and non-philosophy are not entirely extrinsic to one another, and, in the *Tetralogos, an opera of philosophies* (Paris, Cerf, 2019), Laruelle retrieves philosophy again, but this time forced, supported at once by the generic and the quantum. The 'non-' then disappears in order to give rise to a logic of subjects rising from the cave to the stars, only then to descend gently upon humans in order to show them the musical essence of their lives. Faith is, then, expressed in the human voice. Humans can sing faith without confusing it with belief.

My thanks must go to Boris Gunjevic for having carefully preserved this manuscript, which, according to him, dates from 2012.

Anne-Françoise Schmid
Paris
31 August 2019

Acknowledgements

My thanks, first of all, go to Dr Boris Gunjevic (Westfield House, Cambridge), Liza Thompson, Lisa Goodrum, and Lucy Russell (Bloomsbury), without whom this translation would not have been possible. I am also grateful to the French Department (University of Cambridge) and Trinity Hall for their generous support. My thanks must also be given to Dr Ian James (Downing College, Cambridge), my supervisor, for his sound advice on what makes a good translation as well as Professors Anne-Françoise Schmid (EPFL, INSA, INRA, and MinesParisTech) and François Laruelle (Université de Paris-X, Nanterre) for their friendship, hospitality, and support throughout the translation of this book. Finally, my thanks go to Rachel, whose love and patience nourishes all my work.

I dedicate this translation to the memory of Michael, my father-in-law, who passed away during the last week of the translation. Ever interested in my work, Michael would have approached this translation with the simple generosity and intellectual curiosity needed truly to understand a great thinker – an example for any reader. Whether we succeed or not is another matter …

Translator's note

The richness of *Clandestine Theology* cannot possibly be captured in such a short note, so I have drawn together in what follows the most salient aspects that touch upon wider questions in contemporary philosophical and theological debates. I discuss the primacy of faith over belief, the primacy of the Risen over the resurrection, and the Word of the Stranger-subject in order to draw an outline of Laruelle's posture of faith as a generic site for future invention. But I do not, for example, discuss creation, grace, or the relation between the Father and the Son, even though these are also important terms for Laruelle's 'clandestine' theology. I have tried to write a note that interests not only the reader new to Laruelle but also readers more familiar with his work. Where possible, I have avoided using the more abstruse and technical vocabulary in the hope that whatever is lost in precision is compensated by a more accessible introduction. My wager is that the book itself will offer the needed precision and introduce, through its performance or practice, the full sense and scope of technical terms.

Introduction

Laruelle's engagement with Christianity and, more broadly, religion forms part of a wider 'non-philosophical' or 'non-standard' philosophical project. This is worth discussing, very briefly, before properly introducing *Clandestine Theology*. The non-philosophy project is currently organized into five divisions, ranging from the earliest works in the 1970s up to the present. This book is in the last, fifth division. The impetus for this project – more explicitly at least since the early 1990s – is the extension of the sense and scope of the human as well as the practice of thought in a way that is unbound by the demands of the Greek λογός, the presumed sufficiency of Reason, the endless play of Difference, the Event, and any other means by which thought is made self-sufficient or, in more contemporary parlance, something like 'correlational'.[1] What Laruelle finds problematic about such sufficiency is the way the term 'Man', for instance, is thought solely within the horizon of a particular philosophical, theological, or other discursive position; empirical data, phenomena, the *polis*, and so on form the respective basis upon which each thinks and understands the human. But there is, according to non-philosophy, something irreducible about the very material for thinking the human. The various epithets for the human – man is a rational animal, man is a political animal, man is a believing animal, and other similar formulae – are, for Laruelle, chains that bind it more firmly to a particular 'grammar' or logic, missing, in some sense, its irreducible status. In order to liberate thought of the human from such chains, Laruelle poses a radically immanent notion of 'Man' or 'Man-in-person' that captures this irreducible status. But this focus on the human over and against philosophy causes some, like Ray Brassier, for example, to voice concerns about the resurrection of an essentialist or ontological humanism. This is, however, far from Laruelle's intention. I will discuss this issue in the last part of this note, however, since the means by which Laruelle avoids this old ghost rests upon the theoretical machinery of non-philosophy or non-standard thought that needs to be introduced first.

The formulation of a non-philosophical or non-standard theoretical approach serves not only to defend Man or the Human against the sufficiency of certain discourses within the humanities but also to think otherwise than the self-sufficient discourses of philosophy and theology. In order to formulate this alternative, non-philosophy stands in relation to philosophy like non-Euclidian to Euclidian geometry. The purpose and intent behind the prefix 'non-' in non-philosophy indicates neither a negation (i.e. the refusal, substitution, or overcoming of philosophy) nor a suspension (i.e. the preservation of a mysterious, pre-philosophical element, like Schelling's *Abgrund*), but rather a change in the basic structure of thought. The thinker no longer stands, like the philosopher, above or outside experience, from a 'disembodied' perspective, delineating a particular object, determining its conditions and genesis, assigning it predicates and attributes; rather, thought takes place in a radically immanent 'relation' with its 'object' that is determined, in the last instance, by the Real. This amounts to a '"postural mutation" [and] a change of vector' in the orientation and stance of the thinker that fundamentally alters the way thought decides or determines its object. 'The philosophical decision', writes John Ó Maoilearca, 'can be seen as either a determining, intellectual (disembodied) position or, through reorientation, as a bodily "posture" determined by the Real'.[2] The 'Real' designates this radically immanent and material site for thought. As Laruelle writes: 'posture is more subjective, corporeal, and undivided than position; more internal, spontaneous, and naïve than will and decision.'[3] Terms like 'stance', 'posture', and 'position' are not to be taken as simple metaphors, but much more naïvely as literal descriptors of embodied thought. Posture articulates the naïve fact that 'thought distinguishes itself from the body, but in the last instance the latter does not distinguish itself from the former', as Marjorie Gracieuse writes, 'such is the reason why the body … is the real essence of thought'.[4] But non-philosophy does not stand among the numerous philosophies and phenomenologies of the body. The body does not form the object or foundation for a non-standard approach; rather, non-philosophy is a rigorous theoretical apparatus that assumes a radically immanent, material posture of thought.

In order really to effectuate this mutation in a theoretical discourse, Laruelle's non-philosophical project replaces some of the most fundamental philosophical principles with experimental axioms. The correlation between thought and reality, illustrated most clearly in the classical Parmenidian formula that equates the λογός with being (λογός = being), for example, is suspended in favour of an ensemble of axioms and theorems that 'model' the Real. This places Laruelle's work in close proximity to the current 'speculative realist' movement in French and American philosophy that works on the basis that there is no sufficient or adequate 'correlational' relationship between thought and reality, but that the latter remains nevertheless thinkable as such. There are many permutations of this position that I do not wish to discuss here.[5] What sets Laruelle apart, however, is the way in which the non-philosophy project treats and engages with the thought of the Real through philosophy and theology. They are not so much philosophical positions to be engaged with in the *agonistic* struggle that defines philosophical debate, but material for a 'non-standard' mode of thinking. Despite the audacity of Laruelle's non-philosophical or non-standard project, no genuine war is waged, no polemic inveighed, at least insofar as no *position* is taken against this or that philosophy; rather, philosophy becomes the 'material' for a non-standard approach in order to model the Real and its affects in thought.

This highly unusual approach has, however, posed problems for the reception of non-philosophy within the Anglophone academic community, with some, like Graham Harman, for example, holding the view that non-philosophy takes philosophy alone for its object in a way not dissimilar to Derridian deconstruction.[6] In doing so, non-philosophy seemingly reinforces the conviction that thought is bound only to itself, ceaselessly reflecting upon itself, with no outside. Non-philosophy, then, according to Harman at least, repeats the same gestures and peculiar obsessions of the post-war French intellectual scene. But this is not quite the case. While Laruelle does, indeed, engage with key thinkers for post-war French philosophy, like Nietzsche, Hegel, and Heidegger,[7] Harman's view is a little hasty and misleading. It must be understood that nothing could be more anathema to Laruelle's project than simply taking philosophy for its object and reflecting endlessly upon it. Philosophy is not the proper objects of non-philosophy; rather, non-philosophy treats philosophy as one material, among a number of others (theology, photography, and so on), for theoretical experimentation that always concerns the Real and the affects this has upon thought, never philosophy itself. There is no concern with the conditions, whether material, transcendental, or differential, for philosophy, or even its limits, only the radical immanence of the Real. On this fundamental point, Laruelle stands apart from most of his contemporaries (Deleuze, Derrida, and so on) and, in fact, much closer to speculative realism.

The basis for this separation is subtle yet remains crucial for understanding non-philosophy. A non-philosophical 'treatment' of philosophy seeks to measure the mutations that take place within a given philosophical apparatus when its operators, concepts, and syntax are put to the test of the Real and come to model its affects within thought. In this regard, there is some common ground between speculative realism and non-philosophy. But the posture taken by Laruelle with respect to the real differs from many speculative realists: there is no effort to capture the disarray of reality in a series of speculative gestures, no effort to represent or reflect the 'reality' of the Real, through the formulation of functions, objects, and hyper-objects, for example, only the patient, rigorous, and uncompromising mapping out of the disruptive affect radical immanence has upon a particular discourse, whether philosophical, theological, or some other discipline. There is a rare patience, humility, and rigour to non-philosophy that is very much needed for contemporary speculative thought. Laruelle is a scientist measuring the affects of the Real, not some high-flown 'inventor' in a workshop. The 'wildness' of the non-philosophical approach stems precisely from this unyielding rigour and patience.

Both speculative realism and non-philosophy operate in the wake of a broken Parmenidian formula. In a similar way to speculative realism, then, Laruelle's approach means that many normal and well-motivated assumptions held within the horizon of post-Kantian philosophy must be put to one side. Terms like 'transcendental', the 'One', and the 'Real' are set within a very different theoretical framework from Kantianism, Platonism, and even psychoanalysis. The assumption that Laruelle changes most profoundly is the 'originary bilateral continuity' between sensation and understanding that is operated, for example, by the imagination (Kant) or organized by the Will to Power (Nietzsche). This simply no longer holds in non-philosophy. There is no presupposed continuity or parallel between sensation and other empirical data, on one side, and the transcendental, on the other; in short, the bond or correlation between subject and world is broken. The 'miraculous' coincidence of the two is no longer organized and distributed by another term, for example, the transcendental subject (Kant), the Will to Power and the Eternal Return (Nietzsche), the 'plane of immanence' (Deleuze), and so on. Any presupposed unity or bond between terms, whether organized according to unity or even difference, is viewed as philosophy's torsion, twist, or bending back upon itself in order to produce a specular sufficiency that does not *really* hold. What Laruelle poses, instead, is a unilateral duality that organizes and distributes terms within non-philosophy according to the indifference of the Real with respect to all that differs from it.

Difference mutually determines differing terms in a bilateral relation. A difference between terms often affects each in a reciprocal way – for example, an object x is bigger than y and, conversely, object y is smaller than x. But a unilateral difference suspends their reciprocal relation: only a single term differs, with the other term remaining indifferent. 'Lightening, for example', writes Gilles Deleuze, when explaining this kind of difference, 'distinguishes itself from the black sky but must also trail it behind, as though it were distinguishing itself from that which does not distinguish itself from it'.[8] The lightening flashes across the sky, but it alone differs. In the same way, the Real – the 'black sky' in this case – is never affected by difference and remains ever *outside* such relations *at the same time as* being immanent to them. But, unlike Deleuze, this is not 'difference itself' distinguishing itself in a unilateral way. On the contrary, difference does not organize and structure non-philosophy, only the Real. They are contiguous with one another, with the Real always determining in the last instance the posture, gesture, and, ultimately, the identity of thought. The way Laruelle articulates this contiguity is through the idea of the 'clone'. It is not possible to represent the Real – this is ruled out by the rupture in the correlation between thought and reality – but it remains, importantly, thinkable. Thought, therefore, cannot 'copy' the Real, like a Platonic copy or *phantasm* of an Idea, but can, instead, through a non-philosophical or non-standard operation, *clone* it. This ought to be understood in a literal, almost naïve, way: a clone is a copy that does not affect, represent, or present an image of the original; it is an identity in its own right, determined in the last instance by the Real.

The idea of the clone and the operation of clonage articulate a way of thinking a non-sufficient relation between thought and the Real.[9]

What needs to be outlined now is the operation by which clones are produced. This operation is called 'dualysis'. This is Laruelle's response to a unique challenge posed by his non-philosophical posture of thought. Without the supposition of adequacy and lacking any principle of unity, images, or representational ideas, the affect of the Real cannot be brought about and measured by analysis. The reason that analysis does not suffice, put in the simplest terms, is that this concerns always the decomposition of a given object, idea, or entity, into the smallest possible elements. This approach supposes already the unity of the given thing that is apt to be broken down into its component parts *as well as* a unifying operation that gathers these elements together into an object, substance, or entity of some kind. A dualysis, by contrast, takes certain 'elements' – key concepts, operations, and ideas – and lifts them out from their respective conceptual edifice, setting them, instead, in a unilateral relation with the Real. This 'lifting' of ideas, concepts, and figures, out from their conceptual apparatus, is precisely the operation whereby clones are produced. A non-standard thought of a given object no longer seeks to represent or adequately account for its unity and various parts or properties but places such philosophical operations and devices (ideas, concepts, and so on) for thinking an object in a radically immanent relation with the Real, through dualysis and clones, in order to break apart their role within supposedly sufficient conceptual scheme and operate, instead, within a new posture of thought. An idea, figure, or concept is thus 'copied' into non-philosophy, as a clone, in order to extend their scope, outside the constrictions and self-sufficiency of their respective philosophical or theological articulation. Rather than being a transcendent act that is done to a set of materials, accounting for their unity and relations, thought thus turns into a performance or act within radical immanence, setting concepts and ideas in a non-sufficient, unilateral relation with the Real.

A clandestine theology

The foregoing helps to introduce the theoretical machinery Laruelle uses to measure the affect of the Real through a clandestine theology. Written at about the same time as *Christo-Fiction* (2014 [French]; 2016 [English]), *Clandestine Theology* could easily be read as a companion text. They are continuous with one another and form a single project: the reformulation of the status of Christ in order to invert theological and philosophical discourse. In *Christo-fiction*, Laruelle seeks to set Christ on a different theoretical footing from more traditional theology that places Him between the Jew and the Greek, that is, between the Old Testament and Philosophy, Revelation and Reason. This new footing sets itself within a radical conception of immanence that rigorously opposes the transcendence of revelation, on one side, and the inscription of a faithful life within the confines of supposedly sufficient philosophical discourse, on the other. Christ is considered irreducible to the Jewish Torah and the Greek λογός. This view is held by a number of theologians to some degree. But Laruelle radicalizes this irreducible status by insisting on the disruptive immanence of Christ, stripping out transcendence, *telos*, horizon, and world – even the image of the 'mystical desert' – from religious and theological discourse in order to set thought in an immanent posture of faith. This posture is a humble and impoverished one, deprived of the usual means to do philosophy and theology. The terms, concepts, and ideas often employed in theology – revelation, the metaphysical unity and identity of the Father and the Son (*homoousion*), and so on – are put to the test of the Real via

Christ. In *Clandestine Theology*, the disruptive affect of Christ comes through a critique of belief *by faith* that un-seats the authority of the Church and dismantles philosophically sufficient articulations of the Trinity in order to produce a clandestine trinitarian thought. This marks precisely the *clandestine* character of this theology that signals at once a dark, hidden side, outside philosophical and theological discourse, and a certain element of sedition that seeks to undermine the authority of such discourses.

The maxim for Laruelle's clandestine theology is no longer '*crede ut intellegas*' (St Augustine) but could, instead, be 'have faith in order to invent'. From the perspective of this theology, faith is not, first of all, ordered by transcendent beliefs and dogmas but is an immanent experience or lived faith. This immanent fidelity comes first. There are no ontological arguments, leaps of faith, or any *itinerarium mentis in Deum* (St Bonaventure) in this book, only the 'unlearnt ignorance' of the faithful subject, as opposed to the theologian's 'learned ignorance', standing beneath the images, concepts, and ideas that comprise philosophical and theological interpretations and accounts of faith. In order to grasp the faithful subject and lift it out from such interpretative approaches, the subject's faith, too, like Christ, must be rendered irreducible to belief, dogma, tradition, λογός, and revelation. The faithful, understood in this way, are no longer sheltered by the sufficiency and consistency of belief, dogma, and theology but cast out, like a stranger in faith.

Clandestine Theology is, then, a manual or handbook for wandering, like a stranger, through philosophy, theology, and religion. This change in posture sets the stage for a 'theoretical liturgy' – probably the most exciting notion found in this clandestine theology. In contrast to the global and transcendent perspective of the theologian, surveying and setting in order the great estate of the Catholic tradition, the 'clandestine theologian' conjures from this same material (i.e. dogmas, metaphysics, history), through a theoretical incantation, new postures and models for *doing* or rather *performing* faith through theology.

A real critique of theology by faith

The theoretical and axiomatic work undertaken in *Clandestine Theology* can be described precisely as a 'real critique' of theology and philosophy. Unlike a transcendental critique, for example, where the philosopher seeks the conditions for the possibility of something (Kant) or deconstruction, which seeks the alterity or supplement that at once sustains and unsettles the immanent closure of a given system or text (Derrida), a *real critique* subjects the positive systems, principles, and theses that comprise philosophy and theology to the demands of a radical formulation of immanence that suspends their sufficiency and presumed consistency in the way described above in the introduction. Laruelle's immanence thus differs from others – like Deleuze and Badiou – insofar as there is no single governing principle, model, or term that suffices to reflect (in thought) the content of immanence, like difference, diff*er*ance, and event.

Few contemporary philosophers and phenomenologists escape unscathed from Laruelle's real critique. Whether they are named directly or not, Alain Badiou, Michel Henry, Emmanuel Levinas, Jean-Luc Marion, and Jean-Luc Nancy find themselves subject to this real critique in one way or another. The principal focus of this critique from the outset is, however, Badiou's mathematical ontology. Written only a few years after the publication of *Anti-Badiou* (2011), the opening passages of *Clandestine Theology* criticize Badiou's mathematical ontology and philosophy of the event. The motivation for this criticism stems, in part at least, from their proximity. Both Badiou and Laruelle are avowed philosophers of the Real and develop a philosophy that maintains its autonomy and immanence. But this is not the narcissism of small differences. What separates them is a fundamental difference in the way they each configure the relation between thought and the Real. Badiou organizes the Real within a mathematical ontology, using set-theory. Mathematics is the sole medium through which the Real can be made intelligible. Laruelle, by contrast, organizes and articulates this via the generic and axiom-symbols. The theoretical milieu in which non-philosophy operates is not, then, mathematical sets and the void, but rather a mid- or sub-zone called the 'generic'. Like the term 'clone' (above), the generic is best understood, at least initially, in a straightforward manner: the general, generic, or non-specific. As Laruelle explains:

> the generic can be understood, from the outset, in the sense employed in pharmaceuticals and the sciences, where certain properties assume a universal yet not explicitly totalising extension as discrete individuals. This is done either to replace specific or technical names, particularly with respect to a medicine (like a 'label' or commercial name – that is, a *generic* name for a drug) or, in the case of science, redistribute them throughout a number of other disciplines. The generic founds, then, a certain univocity, without forming an explicit totality, being extended throughout a number of disciplines and fields.[10]

The generic stands mid-way between the Being of beings, on one side, and the One, on the other, operating in a no man's land of philosophy. In order to think in this milieu, Laruelle uses axiom-symbols to make gestures and cuts into immanence that remain nevertheless a part of this immanent generic field or sub-zone. While Badiou believes the Real can be ordered to an ontology of the event that finds clear, rational articulation in set-theory, Laruelle refuses any identification between the Real and a particular ontology or mode of intelligibility.

As said, both Badiou and Laruelle share the view that the Real is immanent and autonomous. However, unlike Badiou, Laruelle considers that the content of this autonomous Real does not suppose in any way a 'meta-language' or 'meta-ontology' that could be articulated in a set-theoretical ontology but rather remains materially or linguistically reduced. The Real is foreclosed to language. This follows from the rupture in the identity between thought and being. Each and every theorem, model, axiom, and so forth is subordinate in the last instance to the Real. There is thus a key difference in the way they each understand the relation between the Real and the Name. Symbols or Names are, for Laruelle, linguistically 'reduced' theoretical acts, that is, signs made, not to refer or identify a 'thing' or 'event' but rather to make a cut into immanence. They are intended as *interventions* or *gestures*, rather than a philosophical means to distribute events, subjects, and multiples or sets. They are not posed as exceptions to the Real, that is, performed or enacted from a transcendent position, as if from *outside*, but rather remain immanent in the Real through a unilateral relation. Unlike Laruelle, however, Badiou must pose the empty set or the void as an *exception* in order to articulate the 'multiple of multiples' – that is, the multiple diffusion of sets – and bind together or 'suture' Being and the Name in a coherent ontology. This is a gross simplification, of course, but the critical point still stands. The void becomes the name of Being – the name forming the material content of Being itself.[11] Despite avoiding the danger of binding the two terms together in a restricted materialist ontology, the 'rationalism' underpinning Badiou's mathematical and set-theoretical approach repeats, from Laruelle's non-philosophical perspective, the equation 'thought = being'. 'The intrinsic auto-intelligibility of mathematics, along with the fact that being and thought are the same', writes Laruelle on Badiou's mathematical ontology, 'forms an ontological proof that conforms to the *Parmenidian* matrix'.[12] The introduction of the 'empty set' or 'void' in Badiou's mathematical ontology arrives like a *deus ex machina* at the end of a Greek tragedy, binding all the disparate elements together again.

In contrast to the rationalism and auto-intelligibility of a material and mathematical ontology as well as the dramatic structure of the transcendent intervention *ex machina*, Laruelle employs symbols and axiom like cuts within the radical immanence of the Real, that is, gestures or poses made in immanence. Each symbol or axiom, understood precisely as a theoretical act or cut, produces effects through their concatenation within a particular theoretical apparatus, like an 'installation' (art) or 'experiment' (science), not so much producing transcendent knowledge about an external object than yielding radically immanent knowledge in and through its performance. In contrast to philosophy and theology, for example, Badiou's mathematical ontology, each theoretical cut is never confused with the Real: '[it] is neither of the order of Being, Event, Decision, Cut nor Memory'.[13] On the contrary, the foreclosure of the Real to language and thought, in the last instance, is rigorously maintained as the most minimal axiom for non-philosophy.

The posture of faith Laruelle outlines in *Clandestine Theology* describes this fidelity to the foreclosure of the Real. 'No one "has" or "is" faith', writes Laruelle, 'it is never an attribute or supplement that could be ascribed to an entity, rational or not'.[14] This forms the basis for a critique of belief, dogma, theology, and so on, by faith. The minimal axiom sets theology and philosophy in a subordinate position with respect to the Real. This means that faith is thereby 'sterilized' of any ontological, philosophical, or theological content – that is, cut out from any system or totality that organizes faith into beliefs, dogmas, concepts, and ideas – and set firmly within the 'lived' of faith: Fidelity does not decline from concepts or beliefs, but rather from the the life of the subject. Faith is neither adherence to a *credo* (i.e. transcendent beliefs) nor a mediation between terms (God and the soul), but an immanent posture. This is a posture assumed or taken in the Real, and Laruelle expresses this through the appellation 'in-Man' or 'in-Person' to indicate the radical immanence of this stance. But Man is not, importantly, the same as the subject, like a 'thing' or entity. The name 'Man' designates this 'posture' where the subject stands in faith. But no act, thought, image, or gesture could ever bring about, equate to, or exhaust the thought of Man. In this way, the name 'Man' articulates the foreclosure of the Real at the level of the human.[15] In the context of theology, the faithful posture shifts the centre of gravity away from the sufficiency and totality of a dogma towards the faithful human. Faith concerns immanence, not transcendent beliefs or authoritarian uses of dogma.

> If position is doctrinal, then posture is properly or most radically human, but furnished with a simple alterity or otherness in a unilateral manner ... Faith is not a unity, integrating a multiplicity into a union; it is an identity with a simple "Other than... side or aspect, and is, therefore, more originary than philosophical belief".[16]

The 'simplicity' of this alterity designates a truncated form of philosophical transcendence, that is, a transcendence with only a single movement, without turning or twisting back upon itself, and complements the unilateral difference or duality described above in the introduction. Philosophical transcendence does, however, involve a twist or turn back. This turning back upon itself can be seen, for example, in the Husserlian account of meaning intention, where the transcendent movement of intentionality, moving from consciousness to an object in the world, does not set out simply alone and uncoordinated but turns around an ideal meaning content that consciousness *intends* to express. When an intention is uttered in a propositional statement, that is, precisely *expressed*, the intentional movement is doubled: the first movement is simple transcendence (or intentionality) towards an object in an ordinary, pre-philosophical relation – it is what is *meant* – and the second is a turn back upon this initial movement – reflection, expression, and so forth – in the form of propositional statement (uttered or thought).[17] It is the difference between seeing a red object and stating that something is red. On Husserl's account, the ideal content of the latter structures the intentional relation *tout court* through a doubling of ordinary, pre-philosophical intention within an ideal λογός. Other examples of this doubling can be found, of course, in the Hegelian account of the dialectical unfolding of the Absolute as well as philosophical iterations of repetition and habit. In each case, something finds itself doubled once again and incorporated, in some way or another, into a philosophical λογός as a surviving element under a new guise – that is, unified, organized, and redistributed, either through its overcoming and sublation, its repetition, or through its incorporation into a living, embodied habit. Non-philosophical alterity does not, by contrast, require this additional, backward movement. This marks precisely its simplicity and characterizes the radically immanent posture of faith with respect to the Real, whereby the latter, far from being incorporated or gathered together in some way, through a 'doubling' of some kind, in this immanent posture, is, instead, a simple 'other' that bars the auto-sufficiency of philosophical discourse and marks the identity of each instance of faith in the Real.

In contrast to the sufficiency of doctrinal positions in religion, born from a similar reflexive turning back, the posture of faith faces the demand of the autonomous Real precisely as this Other-than ... It is neither an event, like conversion, nor a unifying principle that gathers together and organizes belief(s). Nothing, strictly speaking, happens to the extent that the Real is an 'unworldly' alterity (or Other-than …) that differs from existential or phenomenological alterity. The Real remains foreclosed to phenomenal experience in this way. The unworldly status ascribed to the Real signals its recalcitrance to the world, analysed and reformulated by various philosophical and theological 'logics'. The 'Other-than …' is not, then, a transcendent Other, like Levinas' Face, that punctuates the immanent horizon of subjective horizon, or a 'transcendence in immanence', like Husserlian phenomenology, but rather an immanent alterity articulated through unilateral duality (see above). Understood from this perspective, faith becomes a disruptive and creative act in the midst of theology and a key component in a theoretical liturgy, where the terms that comprise theological discourse are not organized around and gathered together in a unifying principle but rather made non-sufficient according to the radical immanence of the Real.

We are not survivors of the tomb

How does the minimal axiom, posing the autonomy and immanence of the Real, and the introduction of the posture of faith into the Greco-Judaic interpretation of Christianity affect the status of the Gospels? Given the testimonial basis for Christianity, such a question is crucial, touching upon the revelatory nature of the 'new life' announced in the Gospels as well as the meaning of the life of Jesus, namely, the incarnation, Eucharist, crucifixion, and resurrection. By engaging with this question, Laruelle draws the radical consequences of the 'sayings' and lessons of Jesus, turning them into a 'model' for a real critique of theology performed in a posture of faith. As will be seen, Laruelle's response to this question carries important consequences for the relation between the faithful subject and the Risen Christ as well as the status of writing and scripture. In the course of Laruelle's response, the machinery of the real critique is brought to bear upon Michel Henry, on one side, and the Pauline interpretation of the resurrection, on the other.

If fidelity is no longer bound to (historical) events, dogmas, and transcendent beliefs, but rather situated solely in immanence, then the way the stories, teachings, parables, and episodes or stagings recounted in the Gospels are approached needs to change from a given body of transcendent content to an immanent model for interpreting the affects of this immanence for fidelity through Christ. The words of Jesus in the Gospels provide, for Laruelle, formal models for understanding and interpreting the posture of faith. This 'modelling' intervenes in two interpretative approaches to the Gospels, radicalizing the first and inverting the second: the Gospels are understood to be (1) a phenomenological revelation of a new life (Henry) or (2) a dialectical overcoming of death via the resurrection (St Paul). The first reads them as calls to a new life – that is, the 'happy' and 'simple' discourses, for example, 'the lilies of the field, the birds of the air' (Mt. 6. 25–34). The second reads them as reflections on the necessity of death in the passion sequence (the agony in the garden, the crucifixion, the discovery of the empty tomb, and the Risen body of Christ). Both assume some kind of philosophical and theological content, whether an immediate revelation via auto-affection, on one side, or a dialectical operation, on the other. Laruelle puts both approaches to the test of the Real, using the first to lay the ground for understanding the Gospels in terms of a model and, on this basis, shift the emphasis away from death and resurrection, and, in the second, towards the Risen Christ. I will take the approaches of Henry and St Paul and their respective non-philosophical transformation in turn.

In the first 'revelatory' reading, the Gospels announce the immanent self-revelation of Life in the living. Henry draws the phenomenological consequences of the first type of reading through the formulation of a Christian phenomenology of life during the 1990s.[18] This identifies the Word with the self-revelation of Life in the Gospels and the immediate communication of the Word in the living *pathos* of the flesh, without any distances or gap. The content of the Gospels is revealed fully, without any remainder, in Life. This signals a certain proximity between Henry and Laruelle: each situates the subject in a much more radical conception of immanence than their respective contemporaries and interlocutors. Henry strips out intentionality, horizon, and transcendent Being or Revelation, from the condition of appearing, posing, instead, a 'non-intentional' manifestation described in terms of *pathos* and flesh.[19] The immanent 'λογός of life' is opposed by Henry to the transcendent 'λογός of the world' in a way very close to Laruelle.[20] This immanent, non-intentional appearing is the foundation and essence for manifestation *tout court*, leaving the transcendent horizon constitutively empty and groundless, entirely dependent upon the fullness of immanent life. But Laruelle argues that this does not push immanence and its critical potential far enough. Henry inscribes the immanent experience of the flesh within phenomenological passivity, affectivity, and *pathos*, which ultimately founds subjectivity. The radical experience of immanence is 'lost by Henry in immanence itself, understood as simply interiority', writes Laruelle, 'where it vanishes and becomes transcendental'.[21] Henry's critique of philosophical and phenomenological transcendence lapses into yet another transcendental determination of its essence or foundation. With respect to Henry's phenomenological reading of the Gospels (Word = Auto-Revelation), Laruelle's critique follows similar lines. Just as auto-affection produces a 'transcendental thing', so, too, does the identification of the Word, Christ, and the flesh in auto-generative and auto-revelatory Word produce a 'thing'-like content that is bound to an auto-generative relation between the Son and the Father.[22] Laruelle seeks to force any transcendental content or thing-like character of this immanence off its hinges, pushing faith and the Gospels off their philosophical axes. But it is important to note that this 'unhinging' is not a philosophical *operation* applied to the Gospels. They are, for Laruelle, already separated from the sufficiency and consistency of philosophical interpretation. Stripped of the last remnant of phenomenological material (Henry's *pathos* and auto-affective flesh), the Gospels no longer announce the 'simple' and 'happy' message of Life's auto-affection through the Word – that is, a phenomenologically and materially consistent joy – but rather find their measure in the empty tomb. The empty tomb symbolizes, for Laruelle, not only the death and absence of God on Holy Saturday but also, more profoundly, the void left behind *after* the Risen Christ on Easter Sunday. A Gospel 'unhinged' from any transcendent/transcendental content, far from being reduced to nothing, becomes, for Laruelle, models – that is, an arrangement of material and symbols used to yield new insights into, in this case, the sayings of Jesus and the affect of the Risen Christ. A non-philosophical reading of the Gospels is no longer looking for the hidden meaning of the texts, sayings, and parables but rather applying the Word like axioms in order to yield new, experimental knowledge about the human and the humanity of Christ in a posture of faith.

A consequence of this 'unhinging' of the Gospels is an inversion of the Pauline interpretation of the Resurrection. By stripping the Gospels of their transcendent content and transforming them into models, Laruelle can invert the Pauline interpretation, placing, as will soon be seen, the Risen Christ in a position of primacy with regard to the operation of the resurrection. According to Laruelle, the Pauline reading poses death and the resurrection as the axis around which theology turns in the form of a dialectical 'overcoming' of death via the resurrection. 'The apostle idealises Jesus and transforms Him into a model, in a philosophical or Platonic sense (model-copy), rather than an interpretative model for a formal structure', writes Laruelle, 'such an idealising interpretation gives rise to a dialectical or materialist hiatus'.[23] This results in an interpretation of the Gospels in terms of a 'Life as the object of resurrection, passing through the essential moment of death in order to overcome it'.[24] The hiatus is the moment of death necessary for the coming of the resurrection of life in its shadow. This is the promise of the resurrection. Only the withdrawal of the divine, through death on the Cross, makes the survival of life possible; in other words, the death of God is the condition for life. The withdrawal of the divine, however, for Laruelle, does not merely signal the death of God but rather His survival: 'God has suffered the most modern, even too modern, fate: He is a Survivor reduced to silence.'[25] God is not dead – indeed, God never died – but rather limps on as a mute survivor, struck dumb by the supposed sufficiency of philosophy and theology. God is thus reduced to the 'cadaverous state' of the survivor, placed by Laruelle alongside Absolute Subjectivity (Hegel) and the 'man' of humanism (Feuerbach). This only serves to highlight the impotence of such responses to the nihilistic withdrawal of the divine and the death of God in philosophical and theological discourse; God, life, and the human owe their survival solely to an abstract philosophical operation.

A clandestine theology seeks to invert, not reverse, the survival of God. In doing so, Laruelle makes the Gospels speak once again, but with a different emphasis: the Risen Christ. When the resurrection is understood as survival, the Risen is set under the condition of an essentially philosophical operation. The key culprit for this subordination is, according to Laruelle, St Paul: 'St Paul is the Apostle who sets the resurrection above the Risen, even above the Lived, placing the operation of the resurrection above the Real and, in doing so, revives belief at the expense of faith', that is, belief in a transcendent operation of the Father through the Son.[26] The Risen Christ is reduced to the (philosophical-dialectical) operation of the resurrection, that is, the 'Great Recuperator' who draws together the Jew and the Greek, Revelation and Logos. On this view, Christ is the death and resurrection of every metaphysics and phenomenology of life, the living, and, most importantly, the *surviving*. The potential derangement of the death of God and the empty tomb is sanitized to some extent by *survival*, understood as the result of a dialectical synthesis. In other words, the passage from life to death (first negation) on the Cross (Good Friday), then the resurrection of life (second negation) passes through the death of God – the moment of total absence and profound nihilism (Holy Saturday) – and, in the end, results in the renewal of transcendence – that is, a survival of the negative (Easter Sunday). The operation of the resurrection is dependent upon the action of a transcendent God, incarnating, emptying, and filling once again finite creation with divine grace. Understood in this way, the death of God on the Cross haunts the resurrection. This twists and bends the Risen Christ back upon itself, turning around the axis of the resurrection, thus reducing Christ and the faithful to the status of ghosts that haunt the earth in the shadow of death. A miserable and deathly sacrificial logic sustains this interpretation, ordering the Glory of Christ to the demands of a dialectical operation. In opposition to this essentially Hegelian interpretation, Laruelle eliminates the philosophico-theological operation of negation: life and death are no longer understood in terms of negation – or, more precisely, 'double negation' – but rather symbolize their 'being-separated' and 'non-worldly' status. 'Death symbolises the being-separated or non-worldly status of life.'[27] Death is not an operation, stealing life away from the world, like a thief in the night, but signals the already separated and unworldly status of life. By describing death in this way, Laruelle links the resurrection (St Paul) with the unworldly immanent words of Life (Henry) in a new and radical way. As Laruelle writes,

> dying to the world is also immanent and does not dialectically contradict life – it does not have its place in the tomb – rather this New Life or *a priori* must die in the eyes of the world, but its death must be 'dead'.[28]

No longer understood as a 'double death' – the survival of the death of death – death is, instead, 'Lived Gloriously' through the Risen Christ, who, from the perspective of a clandestine theology, did not die in order to place life once again under the sign of death (on the Cross) but to signal the separated status of life in Glory. The new life announced by the Words of Life (Henry) and the promise of the resurrection (St Paul) are drawn together and mutated by the affect of radical immanence in the 'New Life' of the Glorious Lived, without any auto-affective/auto-revelatory content or dialectical relation. Consequently, the centre of gravity shifts from the philosophical *operation* of the resurrection towards the Glorious Body of the Risen. In other words, the focus moves from the dialectical operation of a synthesis, whether, unifying, broken, or sustained through repetition, towards the 'operative' presence of the Risen Christ in a dimension of simple alterity (see above), with the empty tomb symbolizing, in some sense, the Real. 'Christ is Risen!' cries out within Laruelle's radical immanence. The faithful subject does not continue to pass through the operation of the resurrection – the transformation is always and already complete 'once, each time' in a posture of faith.

The 'operative presence' of the Risen Christ in a dimension of 'simple alterity' is outlined by Laruelle in terms of 'messianity' or 'futurity'. Like science fiction, the future is present in contemporary works through this futurity. The faithful subject 'lives' the simple presence of the Risen or Glorious Lived in a dimension of messianity or futurality, and the eschatological and futural sense of both terms marks a shift away from a recuperative gesture of the resurrection towards a fully operative model for contemporary thought in the Risen, but in temporal terms this time. But the disruptive affect of the Risen Christ mutates the normal temporal order: the 'arrow of *telos*' finds itself not only reversed in direction but 'subverted' into a 'unirection' that accords in some respects with the notion of simple alterity described above. Laruelle's formulation of messianity or futurality does not, then, have any 'intentional object' or Idea, ordering the movement of this arrow around a single axis, or any direction that could be coordinated through other internal or external terms. This is an 'uncoordinated' movement, with only a single unilateral dimension: a 'rection' or 'unirection' – that is, a movement closer to the geometrical sense of angle or straight line, rather than the moral sense of guidance or rule[29]. This is what the Risen Christ, understood and read in the Gospels as a model for faith, teaches: Man 'sub-tends' the radical immanence of faith in a futural dimension. This '*ur*-chronic' future of the Messiah comes only insofar as actually 'arrived' and 'performed' via a decision of faith, that is, as lived by the faithful subject.[30]

The 'unworldly' character of the Word, drawn out by Henry, and the event of the Resurrection are thus set upon a new footing in a posture of faith. The empty tomb is no longer the site for a dialectical operation, recuperating once again the shattered remains of death, but a symbol of the void, before which stands the Risen Christ in full Glory. This void is the Real, foreclosed to philosophy and theology. The Risen Christ, standing before the empty tomb, thus orders the axioms of the faithful to the Real, not the resurrection. We are, then, not *survivors* of the tomb but subjects performing the Risen Christ by means of messianity and futurity in immanence.

The Stranger-subject and the word

By placing the Risen Christ above the operation of the resurrection, Laruelle returns the faithful subject to their peregrination through the (transcendent and philosophico-theological) world, without horizon, fixed position, or *telos*. This is a 'traversal of transcendence by immanence – the traversal of exteriority by faith',[31] where faith is the immanence, foreign and strange, that traverses the world. Rather than being 'sent', 'thrown', or even 'called', by transcendence, whether divine or ontological, the faithful subject is simply sent or 'missioned' to the world by the radically immanent 'unirection' of Messianity, as an 'unworldly' pilgrim or 'messiah-subject'. Like the medieval Christian image, the subject is a stranger, wandering through a foreign land, but their destination this time is neither Heaven nor God – there is no union or return in this sense. The formulation of an immanent posture of faith rules out in advance any *itinerarium mentis in Deum*. There is no inner journey towards divine transcendence. The coordinates for faith are completely different, ordered this time to the radical immanence of the Man (of) faith.

More than simply a poetic illustration, however, the term 'Stranger' carries a technical sense in Laruelle's non-philosophical or non-standard theoretical machinery. The 'Stranger' designates the at once 'unworldly' character of the faithful subject and the non-synthetic relation between the subject and Man. Both the Stranger and Man are identical in the last instance. But the Stranger, as an iteration of Man insofar as subject, is not equal to and does not exhaust the content of Man. The relation between Man and the Stranger-subject parallels, in important ways, the relation between the Risen Christ and the empty tomb. Man is not the 'essence' of the subject but rather a symbol or name that blocks the recuperation of the subject into a philosophical position and maintains him or her as a stranger, to both philosophy and the world. As Laruelle writes,

> when the subject is really detached from the God-world itself, then no ground or foundation can be any more made upon Man-in-Person, as if upon a God, an essence, or super-essence, since this involves always the same logic – the *beyond* man-animal or the *over*-man.[32]

The real critique of the resurrection by the Risen rules out any notion of the beyond- or over-man. This would signal merely the *survival* of the human, whose remnants would somehow live on in such transcendent forms. Man, like faith and the Gospels (above), lacks any transcendent (philosophical and theological) content. There is no substance, essence, transcendent horizon, or world that could provide the material or content for the subject: 'far from seeking within the subject's depths and "nature" whatever might insert this term *a priori* into the transcendence and ends of onto-theo-logy, the humility and solitude of Man is content to exist *according* to its non-essence alone.'[33] The 'Stranger-subject' is thus a stranger to the world as well as to Man – the non-essence of the subject.

Far from reducing the strangers that we are to silence, unable to speak or be heard from within our incarceration in solitude, as arguably Henry's auto-affective life does, the evacuation of any metaphysical, dogmatic, and phenomenological content opens up the theoretical space for invention and experimentation. This underpins Laruelle's transformation of the Gospels into models for a non-theology (indicated above) and rests upon a more radical critique and transformation of the status of writing and scripture. But the reformulation of Messianity or Futurality into a 'unirection' only forms the theoretical basis for a transformation in their status as referential/signifying content for belief. The transformation of the Gospels into models, the inversion of the dialectical interpretation of the resurrection for the benefit of the Risen Christ, and the disruptive affect of Christ in philosophy and theology, taken together, do not yet 'give' voice to fidelity; in other words, they only furnish the conditions for such a change but do not yet transform the referential content for belief into what Laruelle calls the 'uni-voice' (distinct from a univocal λογὸς) of faith.

With the formulation of the 'uni-voice', Laruelle brings the consequences of the foregoing 'real critique' further still, cutting Man and the Stranger-subject loose from the bonds of language. The symbol is an identity that refuses *a priori* any part in the linguistic play of signifier and signification. This stems from the minimal axiom: the Real is autonomous and immanent; therefore, it is foreclosed to language. This limits the way in which language can be employed by the faithful, not in a sceptical manner, as something that cannot ever serve to signify – like a negative theology or *apophasis* – but precisely as an experimental application of terms in order to measure their effects.

There is no adequate relation between language and the Real. A symbol or name cannot exhaust the content of its referent. But the foreclosure of the Real to language does not signal a profound alienation; quite the reverse, in this posture we are free: 'we are definitively free from the chains of language, which have been the instrument of our alienation, and not only in a philosophical manner.'[34] The difference between word and thing no longer serves at once to bind and alienate the subject, not only from and to its object but also from and to itself (insofar as 'object' or 'referent'); on the contrary, the asymmetry between the Real and language breaks even the 'failed' or 'incomplete' synthesis of word and thing and recasts it, instead, according to a unilateral duality that articulates the 'syntax' for the uni-voice.

Just as with the Gospels, Laruelle produces a voice 'unhinged' from language by radical immanence. This completely overturns the status of Writing and Scripture. In monotheistic religions, writing and scripture form an important part of a 'spiritual hermeneutics' of the (natural) world insofar as they stand as the mediating third-term between God and human expressions (revelatory Word) or the One and the Multiple (philosophical λογός). As Laruelle writes, 'the more God is unique and transcendent, the more the book and writing are the single, real support for monotheist religions and the very last mirror for this God.'[35] This forms a 'triadic' structure – God-Book/Writing-World – that produces a series of relays or mediations between God and the Word, the soul and God, the subject and faith, and so on. Each term encroaches upon the other in a circular way, producing a cycle of perpetual slippage from one term to the next. This cycle gives rise to instances of hesitation, pauses, and, in the end, alienation: the soul, passing through language (scripture or writing) and confessing belief in another, yearns for a 'transcendent interiority' – that is, the *Deus interior intimo meo* that organizes the Augustinian tradition seeking union between two terms, namely God and the soul.[36] But the unhinged uni-voice means that there is no possible union, no lost origin, and no immemorial. The antiphony of belief – that is, the call and response between the soul and God in prayer and confession – is replaced by the uni-phony of faith. This means that neither writing nor scripture is any longer understood to be the privileged site for mediation between terms or, indeed, to harbour the Real.

> Rather than attempting to decipher the hidden meaning of the Gospels with the nostalgic air of fundamentalism, either adding or subtracting distance upon distance, and refusing to acknowledge that this is now definitively lost and, more than lost, vanished or absent, wholly missing 'from' the texts, the faithful ought to produce the sense and meaning of the Scriptures in the very act of their transformation, according to the function of the *a priori* of faith.[37]

The Gospels are not the bearers of the real content for faith. They are models (see above). The loss of any dimension of 'hidden' or 'secret' meaning is not understood, then, in the mode of nostalgia but in the mode of production, invention, and transformation, in accordance with the radical immanence of faith. Simply put, the Real that sustains the faithful subject in a posture of fidelity is no longer understood to be housed in or mediated through the foundation of writing or scripture but rather lived and performed in the immanence of the Glorious Lived of Christ:

> with Christ-in-Person, such univocity ruptures at the generic threshold of a non-theology in the form of a uni–voice – the really unique call, without either a caller or respondent. This uni–voice is the ultimatum that forces me, as a speaking and writing subject. It is not God who is unique, but Man. Yet the unicity of Man is no longer numeric or transcendent; rather, Man is unique by being simply in-Man and the voice is unique by being simply in-voice. The heno-phonology signals the 'end' of authoritarian logocentric philosophy.[38]

Contrary to the Pauline, broadly philosophical, interpretation of Christ, the empty tomb does not bind Man and the Stranger-subject to the unifying dialectical operation of the resurrection, subordinate, in the end, to the unity of God the Father, but sets both free as unique, not *before* the Cross but rather in a posture of faith *in* Christ: 'as soon as uniqueness and inalienability, formerly inscribed within the divine, are admitted as immanent and accepted as such, they change their course and Real mode of insertion.'[39] This new mode of insertion is precisely as already *a priori* unique and inalienable, rather than the result of a dialectical synthesis or responsorial ontology. Scripture thus assumes the status of the Risen. It no longer mediates the Word of the unique, transcendent God but speaks out from the void – that is, the immanent posture of faith determined by the Real. This unique and inalienable status undercuts the desire for union that results from the slippages and pauses of the circular relation between God, the Word, and the Subject.

> What does this concern, then, if not to free the Word from the Logos and grant this to Man, instead – this being who has not been created or programmed in order to speak or think solely to be faithful to a logic and a faith, that is, to employ the language of the world?[40]

Man speaks, not on behalf of or mediated through the Divine or the Logos but in a posture of faith. The unworldly and gnostic character of fidelity is free from the horizons of philosophical and theological discourse and, as the lesson of the empty tomb shows, Christ is the force that breaks these chains.

Laruelle and the future of theology: A theoretical liturgy

A clandestine theology describes the struggle of Man via the decision of the Stranger-subject for faith against the constrictions of belief, dogma, and their authoritarian application by the Church. In light of this struggle, I want to offer a few closing remarks on the impact a clandestine theology has upon contemporary theological debates. What follows are a few brief indications where this touches upon the struggle for theology today.

The questions a clandestine theology raises for theology differ, of course, from those of the author. Despite the different questions and problems, the foregoing note outlines a very delicate theoretical machinery that carries radical consequences for the way theology could approach trinitarian metaphysics today. In marked contrast to many other prominent post-war French philosophers and phenomenologists, who so often look to overcome or critique metaphysics, some theorists note that the non-philosophical project promises its liberation and, perhaps, even renewal. According to Katerina Kolozova, for example, non-philosophy initiates the 'emancipation of metaphysics from the authority of philosophy', and, one might add, theology, too, through its radicalization in terms of the last-instance, that is, Man and the Real.[41] It is important to bear in mind that non-philosophy does not seek to supplant or overcome philosophy *tout court* but rather sets in motion the emancipation of metaphysics from the authority of a certain kind of philosophical stance that presumes or seeks to confect self-sufficiency and autonomy from the affect(s) of the Real. But this emancipation is only radical, according to Kolozova, when metaphysics is understood as the 'necessary mediator or core of radical subjectivity', that is, the heart of the Stranger-subject. A non-philosophical radicalization of metaphysics renders this no longer to the service and benefit of philosophy and theology but for the Stranger-subject and Man.[42] Something similar can be said about a clandestine theology: the 'unhinging' of Man, the Stranger, the Word, and the Risen undertaken in this book performs a parallel emancipation of faith, rendering trinitarian metaphysics to its service, not theology. This impacts directly upon the unity and economy of the Trinity, something that this book announces from the start and addresses directly in the closing chapters of the book. This 'unhinging' is designed to emancipate and preserve the Trinity from the self-sufficiency of its philosophical and theological iterations in order to extend its scope and range for a future theoretical liturgy, putting trinitarian metaphysics to the service of faith and Man, rather than the authority and supposed sufficiency of theology.

The defence of Man against the authority of such philosophical and theological discourses is integral to clandestine theology as well as the non-philosophical project as a whole. But repeated references to such terms like 'Man' and 'Man-in-person' has led some, like Ray Brassier, to criticize non-philosophy for restoring what they see as a humanist ontology or essentialism: 'by insisting that "the human" remains the invariable site of the last-instance [i.e., the Real], Laruelle risks regressing back into Henry's pathetic transcendental egology ... to a transcendental individualism.'[43] The identification of Man and the Real, according to Brassier, surreptitiously restores an ontology or essence of the human that repeats, in some sense, the incarceration of the human in an egology or transcendental individualism. But this rests upon a somewhat misleading premise: the criticism Brassier and others make only holds if the identification of the human as the exclusive site of the Real rests upon a reversible equivalence, whereby Man *is* the Real, Stranger-subjects *are* Man, and *vice versa*. But Laruelle's identification between these terms is asymmetrical; they are not exchangeable with one another. While individuals are equally, in the last instance, determined by the Real, they are not equivalent or exchangeable with one another as a result. This asymmetry and unexchangeable quality results from the unilateral relation (see above) between the human and the Real. Indeed, the asymmetrical identity is the means by which Laruelle performatively instantiates the non-sufficient identity of Man and the Real *as well as* the Stranger-subject and Man in order to broaden the scope and extension of terms like 'Man', 'Man-in-person', 'Human', and so on, beyond the confines of any particular discourse. Such terms are left indefinite and undefined for theoretically rigorous reasons: 'Man only exists as a multitude of Strangers, in a manner that gives meaning again to the old concept of *multitudo transcendentalis* and of posing democracy at the heart of the science of men.'[44] Recall that the 'Stranger' designates both the 'unworldly' character of the subject and the non-synthetic relation between the subject and Man. The Stranger insofar as an iteration of Man in terms of subjectivity does not equal or exhaust Man. The term 'Man' does not, then, designate an ontological or essential property shared by a multitude of subjects; rather, the unilateral relation between Man and Stranger-subjects means that the former names only a series of such strangers. Indeed, the unilateral difference that articulates the indifference of Man and the Real with respect to subjects is precisely what renders subjects strangers to the Real and, indeed, estranged from any determination of 'Man'. The strangeness of each individual with respect to Man and the Real poses precisely the emancipatory democracy of thought that is so crucial to non-philosophy and non-standard thought, paving the way towards the radicalization of metaphysics mentioned above. As John Ó Maoilearca writes, 'individuals *make* equality, they do not possess it (as a philosophical property of difference, multiplicity, etc.).'[45] The determination of each individual (in the last instance) by the Real preserves their relative autonomy with respect to philosophical and theological determinations, including humanism and transcendental egology, and thereby prevents the sort of ontological or essentialist restoration of humanism that Brassier rightly warns against. The indefinite status of Man and individuals is precisely the means by which Laruelle defends them against the authority of philosophical and theological forms of humanism and poses, instead, a genuine democracy of non-philosophical or non-standard thought, rendering philosophy and theology, through techniques like 'cloning' and 'dualysis', to the service of a radical subjectivity, as Kolozova suggests.

A clandestine theology continues in this vein through its formulation of the posture of faith according to the Risen Christ. The 'unhinging' of the Risen from the operation of the resurrection, the Word from the Book, and so on, undertaken in this book, makes each individual a stranger in faith. The authority of theology is thereby undermined for the benefit of the lived faith of the stranger.

A clandestine theology offers thus a curious defence of the Trinity and intervenes precisely where it teeters on the brink: 'the Trinity', writes Laruelle, 'is the ridge or precipice *par excellence*, where thought can topple from theology down into philosophy once again or be reduced to an *a priori* human, real, and, therefore, a transcendental content'.[46] From the perspective of a non-philosopher, the Trinity needs sheltering from the menaces of philosophy, especially dialectical logic ('Hegelianism ... menaces all philosophy and theology'). Such shelter and protection are found by placing the Trinity in the service of the faithful subject and thinking it within a posture of fidelity. There is always the risk that the Trinity will lapse into philosophical sufficiency and consistency, silencing the faithful subject and replacing it with a believer, who is now subject to the demands of a particular extrinsic theologico-philosophical discourse. A clandestine theology offers some of the tools needed to keep the Trinity from teetering over this edge and, instead, draw it back towards the human real.

In doing so, *Clandestine Theology* revives an almost forgotten theological insight. Often the Trinity functions precisely like a transcendent machine, ordering faith to beliefs, dogmas, and a certain dialectical logic, supplanting the inconsistency of lived faith for the consistency and sufficiency of philosophy and theology. But it is the reverse: Man, standing in a posture of faith, *precedes* the metaphysical articulation of the Trinity. This is one of the lessons to take from a clandestine theology. A lived faith is not subject to metaphysics and theology but finds its expression therein. The great works of the Church Fathers (Ireneus, Tertullian, amongst others) and the Medieval period (St Bonaventure, St Aquinas, Meister Eckhart, amongst others) were understood by their authors as expressions of faith in metaphysical and theological prose.[47] The modern distinction between the construction of a theoretical system or metaphysics and a spiritual life of faith is, as Pierre Hadot notes, simply not made within their works.[48] They are products of a lived faith, expressed and articulated precisely within a certain posture of faith. A clandestine theology seeks to radicalize this insight through the Risen Christ. The immanent posture of faith intends to put the 'standard' or 'norm' to the test of the disruptive affect of the Real through the Risen Christ. This disruptive and unhinging affect is the true standard that measures any thought of the Trinity, not the reverse. With this 'non-standard' model, the metaphysical edifice of the Trinity articulates a Christian lived, spiritual experience, with the latter nourishing the former in a speculative exposition of a living faith, according to a radical democracy of thought.[49]

But a clandestine theology goes further still. Laruelle refuses any possible sufficiency or consistency between faith and speculative trinitarian metaphysics, setting them both in a dimension of radical immanence that is articulated through a posture of faith. This refusal maintains and insists upon the disruptive and unhinged faith of a clandestine theology that echoes the 'madness of Christ' described by Stanislas Breton.[50] Christ is Risen not only in order to overcome death and fulfil the promise of a new life but also to invert and determine faith. Between the rational theology of St Thomas, on one side, and existential theology of Rudolf Bultmann, for example, on the other, stands the maddening effect of the Cross. Neither, according to Breton, adequately captures the radicality of the Christ on the Cross.[51] An account of the Trinity can be made to express this radicality and madness precisely through a faith unhinged, and a clandestine theology provides the machinery for a 'theoretical liturgy' or 'poetics' that starts from this deranged point.[52] But there are, of course, differences between Breton and Laruelle. The former rests his attention upon the moment of fracture and disruption on Good Friday, holding philosophy and theology together in the tension of this instant, the latter, the promise this fracture holds for a future theology on Easter Sunday. Put another way: the former rests upon the *break* and *fracture* within philosophical and theological sufficiency, while the latter sets the Risen in front of this break, in front of the empty tomb, opening up a futural dimension for non-standard theological thought, determined always in the last instance by the Real.

What does all this mean for 'standard' theology and the tradition? *Clandestine Theology* offers a means with which to subordinate this suggested theoretical liturgy of the Trinity to the autonomous and immanent Real (the minimal axiom) of faith and thereby cuts it loose from the bonds of the sufficient and transcendent use of dogma and tradition. But this does not simply negate or suspend them; rather, it treats them as material and measures them according to the disruptive affect of the Risen Christ. In a posture of faith, theology measures itself against the mutating affect of Christ. This does not mean that the tradition is in some way set to one side but rather employed as material for a theoretical liturgy that concerns itself more with invention than convention. Far from casting theology into a romantic and mystical cloud of unknowing, however, the non-philosopher's confession of faith opens a way towards restoring the dignity of thought and the production of a new knowledge in a posture of faith. This posture embraces the 'madness' and unhinged effect of the Risen Christ on supposedly rational, speculative articulations of the Trinity: 'the Risen is non-reason, without being irrational.'[53] In other words, the Risen is irreducible to philosophico-theological interpretation but remains nevertheless thinkable, demanding its own form of 'non-reason' or a 'non-standard' model of rationality. 'Non-reason' does not, then, mean un-reason. This last point is key: the suspension of the dialectic does not plunge philosophy and theology into a Schellingian abyss or a maddening Nietzschean vicious circle. This is not a declaration of the 'end of philosophy' or the 'end of theology' in favour of chaos. The alternatives 'rational or irrational' and 'reason and sensation' are operative only in philosophy and a certain kind of philosophical theology. A clandestine theology is neither a positive, traditional theology nor a purely negative and impotent a-theology. Rather, Laruelle furnishes contemporary theology with the theoretical means to suspend such false alternatives that cut into the very fabric of fidelity and, instead, turn its attention towards the reality of faith.

In a clandestine theology, fidelity is ordered according to the effects of the 'most minimal axiom' – that is, the radical immanence and autonomy of the Real – and thereby becomes a performance and a liturgy. The articulation of the Trinity in a speculative, theoretical discourse can become like a liturgical practice, not commenting upon or deciding, but living in faith. From this immanent perspective, the act of invention and transformation is the true work of faith, that is, not to possess or to define, but to invent. 'How to be in the world', asks Breton, 'without being of the world? There is no complete answer to this eternally aporetic question, yesterday, today, and always, since we need, each time, to invent, if, that is, it is true that faith is never an acquisition or a definitive possession'.[54] This is the concern of a clandestine theology, too. The challenge posed by Laruelle's confession of faith is not to *possess* or *acquire* faith that is always *of* this world but to assume a *posture* of faith that invents, once and each time, a living fidelity that is *out of this world*. We, the 'without-religion', are called to be no longer mere subjects but rather strangers in faith; each performance of this faith, in a theoretical liturgy, is a step out upon an earth that only materializes once our feet strike the ground – the miracle of a clandestine theology.

Andrew Sackin-Poll,
Trinity Hall, University of Cambridge
14th December 2019

References

Brassier, Ray, *Nihil Unbound: Enlightenment and Extinction* (London: Palgrave Macmillan, 2007)

Breton, Stanislas, *Le Verbe et la croix* (Paris: Mame-Desclée, 2010)

Deleuze, Gilles, *Difference and Repetition*, trans. by Paul Patton (London: Continuum, 2004)

Falque, Emmanuel, *Dieu, la chair, et l'autre, D'Irénée à Duns Scot* (Paris: PUF, 2008)

Gracieuse, Marjorie, 'Laruelle Facing Deleuze' in *Laruelle and Non-Philosophy*, ed by John Mullarkey and Anthony Paul Smith (Edinburgh: Edinburgh University Press, 2012)

Hadot, Pierre, *Exercices spirituels et philosophie antique* (Paris: Études augustiniennes, 1981)

Henry, Michel, *I Am the Truth*, trans. by Susan Emanuel (Stanford: Stanford University Press, 2002)

Henry, Michel, *Material Phenomenology*, trans. by Scott Davidson (New York: Fordham University Press, 2008)

Henry, Michel, *Words of Christ*, trans. by Christina Gschwandtner (Michigan: Eerdmans Publishing Company, 2011)

Henry, Michel, *Incarnation: A Philosophy of the Flesh*, trans. by Karl Hefty (Evanston: Northwestern University Press, 2015)

Husserl, Edmund, *Ideas Pertaining to a Pure Phenomenology and to a Phenomenological Philosophy*, trans. by F. Kersten (The Hague: Martinus Nijhoff, 1982)

Kolozova, Katerina, *Toward a Radical Metaphysics of Socialism, Marx and Laruelle* (New York: Punctum, 2015)

Ò Maoilearca, John, 'The Animal Line, On the Possibility of a "Laruellean" Non-Human Philosophy' in *Angelaki: Journal of the Theoretical Humanities*, vol 19, no. 2 (June 2014)

Ò Maoilearca, John, *All Thoughts Are Equal: Laruelle and Non-Human Philosophy* (Minneapolis: University of Minnesota Press, 2015)

Laruelle, François, *Théorie des Étrangers* (Paris: Éditions Kimé, 1998)

Laruelle, François, *Introduction au non-marxisme* (Paris: PUF, 2000)

Laruelle, François, *Philosophy and Non-Philosophy*, trans. by Anthony Paul Smith (London: Bloomsbury, 2017)

Introduction

Contrary to Alain Badiou, there is an immanent knowledge that is not mathematical. Badiou is right, however, to refuse the mixture of the infinite and finite, but the finite remains, for us, nevertheless a *mediation* – something he refuses in favour of an infinite void of the subject. The materialism Badiou sets forth poses the infinity of mathematical material alongside an arbitrary nomination that hangs nothing on the infinite itself. This reduces the infinite to nomination, while the subject remains an infinite mediation, whether immanent or immediate. It seems that Badiou is, then, as much a gnostic about mathematics as I am about Man, but a gnostic materialist, according to the equation mathematics = ontology.

Clandestine theology: The impossible *homoousia* and the destruction of the trinity

If *homoousia* is made impossible, if the co-substantiality of the Father and the Son is rendered inoperative, then this would mark the destruction of the Trinity. The principle of Christology is, of course, the consubstantiality of the Father and the Son, that is, *homoousia*, and this makes the Trinity and the circulation of the Divine Persons possible. It is very clear that co-substantiality breathes substantiality – co-physism is indebted to physism, if not mono-physim, and so on. In place of this principle we pose uni-substantiality, which is not a 'single' substance or a 'one', possessing only unity and sameness, but the non-substance of the Real. This non-substance sub-tends the Trinity, not as a subject, bearing predicates and attributes, but as generic futurality – that is, as the half-presence of unilateral duality. This grants a place to Being, but only insofar as a clandestine half-presence or non-substantial *a priori*. Whether or not the *ousia* in *homoousia* presupposes an un-interrogated sense of Being that is thematized only for itself matters little. Without this clandestine substitution, we would hardly advance at all. What matters most here is that Being insofar as it is *not* axiomatized in a fiction, according to the One, contains and shelters a pre-decided and possibly deconstructible theology, whereas neither theology nor deconstruction satisfies us. They must both undergo a dualysis that reduces them to the status of a model for a non-Christian thought. With this clandestine substitution, the Parmedian equation (Being = Thought) that forms the matrix of *homoousia*, posing the sameness of the Father and the Son, with a few reservations, of course, but also a certain mark of their convertibility – "who has seen the Son has seen also the Father" (Jn. 14. 8–10) – must undergo a dualysis, too.

An axiomatic of the trinity

Once again the dismantling of the Trinitarian equation (that requires only the Father or Man be said 'in-person', while other terms are called so only according to Him) supposes that the Trinity, posited as the dogma of dogmas or the founding axiom of Christianity, possesses the genetic power of a theorem. This, in turn, supposes that the entirety of Christian life can be deduced from the mixture of the Father and

Man; in other words, the Trinity is supposed to be a theorem that can be obtained through the addition of an axiom to these two terms, that is, a synthesis of an empty axiom and a reversible theorem (Father = Son). The Trinity must not be understood in terms of an axiom, which is contingent and could be withdrawn, but rather deduced under new conditions, namely from the most minimal axiom: the Real as immanent and autonomous (like Badiou's mathematics).

Such minimal axioms are posed retroactively by the Stranger-subject or Messiah and will be called an 'axiom-fiction' that is performed by the work of the Messiah-subject. They are as follows: (1) the Real of Man is posed as immanent or autonomous, with God forming the most proximate image or model; (2) the immanence and autonomy of Man is foreclosed to theological thought and language. As immanent in-the-last-instance, the axiom-fiction of the non-religious Real is empty of all religious content, even the infinite of transcendence, meaning that the significance of emptiness = an impossible *a priori*, but remains nevertheless full of theological materiality in the form of an *a priori* given or *datum*.

This axiomatic of Man or the Real is necessary and completely foreclosed to theological thought and language. The axiom of the non-religious Real is devoid of any religious content. Even the void at the heart of Emmanuel Levinas's phenomenology, where 'emptiness = impossible *a priori*', is still full of a theological materiality. The axiom that is 'empty-of' theology (i.e. Man without-Theology), whereby the operator 'empty-of' is understood in terms of an engaged void – that is not at all an absolute, like Badiou, yet possesses a material content – must be separated from the theorem that supposes a *sufficient* content, thus distinguishing this theorem from the ultimate difference between sufficient material and reduced matter, which is sufficient philosophy, understood as a simple modelling. Axioms are neither formal, material, nor ontologico-intellectual, that is, intuitive. Rather, they have an *a priori* materiality.

The same distinction could hardly be less crudely stated for materialism, for example, mathematizing or set-theorizing, than for Christian theology. In both cases, the question of dogma appears at the end, only after the axioms of Greek ontology and set-theoretic axioms have been developed. A mathematical-positive or set-theoretic content supposes a meta-language or philosophical 'meta-ontology', while axiom-fictions are, by contrast, materially or *a priori* linguistically reduced, never sufficient. But the ontological content of Badiou's axioms (or theory of sets) is mathematical, supposing a philosophical meta-language, while my axioms are linguistico-materialistic or philosophically reduced, and so *non*-sufficient. Is this not the same thing? In short: no. Badiou must add an empty set and claim that *the void is the name of Being*. This is very important: it means 'Being' is no longer a philosophical name but a thing or an instance, and its name – the 'void' – forms, in some sense, the suture of Being (the Real) and the void (the Name). The void is *the name* of Being – Being is a philosophical or meta-ontological name. But the *a priori* materiality of a name is fully a phenomenon. The name 'void' is the material content of Being itself. But this does not form a straightforward suture (a form of simplified and materialistic mixture) of Being (the Real), on one side, and the void (the Name), on the other. This would simply be an attenuated or materialistic form of the ontological argument, that is, the identity of the thing with its name. The intrinsic 'auto-intelligibility' of mathematics, verging on the meta-ontological, means that Being and thought are the same, forming a Two that is not identical in-the-last-instance, only identical with the One of Being.

What Badiou puts forward, then, is a new ontological argument, asserting the identity of the name and the thing. Nothing is emptier than the void or empty set. This turns the empty set into the 'God of mathematics'. This is a very philosophical way of arguing – the void is the name of the language of Being! The intrinsic auto-intelligibility of mathematics, along with the fact that being and thought are the same, forms an ontological proof that conforms to the *Parmenidian* matrix. In the face of this ontological proof that Platonizes materialism, carrying within itself its own intelligibility – the very action of immanent transcendence – I oppose the radical immanence of gnosis as an 'un-learnt' knowledge that does not make any leap out from the ontological argument. We must choose between the ontological leap and immanent knowledge, whereby the axiomatic 'cut' must come second in relation to immanence, posited within the element of an *a priori* and certainly not to be confused with the Real. While for Badiou mathematics forms its own discourse, non-philosophy distinguishes the Real and knowledge of the Real, on one side, which guarantees the immanence of this discourse, and philo-fiction as a discourse or matter and symptom of axioms, on the other.

The empty set of Badiou's ontology is as miraculous as the 'Son of Man' formula! If the formula 'Son of Man' is taken literally, then, from this point of view, there is no Father and all human beings are empty. What this means is that emptiness, that is, the Son, is the name of all humans – the whole of humanity. This is an interpretation according to the ontological proof! But for us, by contrast, the same formula means that there is no set (the function of humanity): there are humans – or there is Man – but this does not form a whole or totality, and so the Son refers to Man (i.e. the Real of Man; i.e. 'in-Man' or 'in-person'), not God. Our interpretation refuses the theologico-familial metaphor: the Son is not the name of God and He is Himself a Man and, therefore, a Son-*without*-filiation. The Son is the name of Man, while remaining distinct from the latter. This will be set and articulated within a special form of axioms for a non-philosopher's confession of faith.

This non-philosophical confession is a non-sectarian thought in the time of sects. Sects form something like a heretico-religious symptom of a war waged against Man. A sect draws together the multiplicity of the Church or Scripture and religious criteria; they engage in sexual, psychological, and financial exploitation similar to the Church, but under a sharper, more visible form. This is the heretico-religious: a bad mixture of heresy, abstract philosophical divisions, and deathly religion. Does the sect not abuse the Divided Real and set this above the Un-divided? Why such an abuse? Why the parody of generic messianity? What a non-philosophical confession performs is an heretical, not parodic, form of generic messianity that does not mimic or ape the empty gestures of philosophical abstraction or deathly beliefs of religion but comes to the defence of Man through a confession of faith in the form of axioms.

1

Faith and belief

Man-in-person as universal *a priori*

I will set the symbols of faith within a special form of axioms that explain and articulate the faith I consider to be precisely the intimacy or immanence of the 'consubstantiality' of Man. Such an intimate faith can only be confessed in the form of axioms, which are empty of their theological sense and meaning but nevertheless employ theological vocabulary. This generic distribution of religion (including structures, dogmas, and beliefs), according to faith, will thus set in motion the particular religion designated by the symbol or first term 'Christ'. On this basis, there is an objective religious appearance – Christian – that is, perhaps, contingent upon a particular confession of faith. The universal generic posture (of faith) – that is, non-philosophy – must now be defined in order to clarify the possible basis for this appearance. Through non-philosophy, the generic nature of faith is discovered in a non-reflected way.

I understand by *Man-in-person* a number of axioms, which, in turn, contain many others. We will thus call (1) the Real as radical immanence (of) Lived, therefore, Lived-without-life or Real-without-reality, separated by axiomatic 'definition' 'from' any and all reality or even 'from' the World; (2) the Real as an *a priori* form – that is, an immanent and lived form – but from the perspective of the World this time, assuring thus that the donation of the World is reduced to its human determination; (3) the Real as the most universal determining instance of knowledge that brings the philosophico-theological structures, which constitute precisely the World-Form *par excellence*, and the World (and not only an isolated content) together in relation.

Man-in-person is a real *a priori*. Man is neither substantial nor in and for itself but rather radically immanent. This forms an identity that is empty of all substance and, therefore, devoid of any subject and attributes. Man is the universal *a priori* for the worldly universal. I call this point of view, comprised of such axioms, 'generic' rather than 'philosophical' on the basis that it 'contradicts' philosophical logic at the same time as making use of its vocabulary. They form neither a meta- nor a para-philosophy; non-philosophy is neither above nor simply beside or adjacent to philosophy; neither philosophy nor topology determines its essence.

Since the Modern Age, the theologico-philosophical form of the World has rested upon the two pillars of faith and mathematics. But the Modern Age results from their premature combination under the authority of philosophy. This leaves us the task of thinking each in terms of an effect of Man-in-person and, subsequently, the determination of a non-theology parallel to a non-epistemology. There are many types of universal and heterogeneous knowledge, each producing their own truths. They emanate from science, art, religion, love, economy, politics, rather than being limited to just four and bound to a single conception of 'truth' or half-truth, even a truth-without-knowledge, with some nuances and variations that form a philosophical system (Badiou). But the generic is something altogether different: it is Truth-without-truth. This should not to be confused with the knowledge of first truths or the truth-without-knowledge of philosophy. The generic should, furthermore, not be taken for a synthesis or complement. It should rather be understood as 'once, each time' the human Identity-in-the-last-instance of philosophy and the truths specific to particular domains of knowledge. We place under the form of the 'non-religious', for example, the generic identity of faith in-the-last-instance along with religion, including every specific religion. Under the form of thought-science, we place mathematics (as *mathesis*, rather than *matheme*), and, therefore, science and epistemology, too. The new experience of non-religion, no longer understood as a predicate of Man but rather a 'post-dicate', adds nothing to the real of faith (i.e. the Real). Non-religion is, therefore, a religious (real-)transcendental; it is simple, like faith, and universal, yet never totalizing or totalitarian, like certain religions. It is simple and non-reflected, without the thickness and density that characterizes the duplicity and complexity of religion.

I admit the possibility of a generic discourse of faith – non-religious or non-theological – that is in accordance with faith. This does not mean absolutely without since such a discourse still uses concepts from theology and history, yet it remains irreducible to them. On the contrary, faith is capable of determining them. Hence, the following axion: *faith is foreclosed to religion but nevertheless determines the religious.* This is more than a clarification of terms, a statement of the situation, or tidying up of logical confusions; rather, this concerns a decision of an axiomatic type, which, in the end, makes possible a 'thought-faith' or a 'non-religious' faith. In this way, a transfer of thought from philosophy or theology to faith is accomplished. This is done in order to liberate faith, which currently lacks its own thought, from the forces that are always and already imposed upon it (i.e. by philosophy and theology). Such a liberation would not banish theology altogether, only suspend its power and supposed autonomy. We have, then, the task of detaching, from one another, the two very slender films or surfaces, seemingly identical or fused together, even contiguous with one another, that constitute the density and sufficiency of spontaneous theology. This transfer takes place in two distinct stages: (1) show that faith is a human 'posture' through and through, and so radically autonomous and foreclosed to religions precisely at the moment when they need faith in order to express themselves; (2) show that theology, reduced to a single film or surface – that is, an appearance, without density or thickness – is necessary for statements determined by faith, giving them an objective religious and worldly form but reduced by faith itself (as a transcendental reduction). Thought, reduced to such a state of transcendental appearance, is thus removed from the ambit of philosophy and redistributed equally throughout its 'regional' or 'non-fundamental' activities. This is only a single moment in an enormous task that introduces a certain democracy into the exercise of thought, although not through a distribution, since democracy is an Identity that is precisely not shared or distributed but rather given. This undertaking amounts to tearing the problem of faith out from religion in order to treat the effects of faith under a form of knowledge and truth – that is, to make faith pass from religious mythologies into a sphere of thought, as thought-faith, alongside thought-science, thus assuming the same privileges as art, economics, politics, and so on. In short, faith leaves the heavens and the earth in order to meet Man precisely where he stands in immanence. This is the age of non-religious faith that has nothing whatsoever to do with modern secularization, which is really only a debasement of the old mythology. The subject (of) faith is the subject 'in struggle', like others and alongside them.

The generic style and its two interpretations

We propose the introduction of what could be called the 'generic' point of view – that is, no longer a philosophical or theological perspective – into religion, in particular Christianity, in order thereby to displace the ensemble of theologico-symbolic apparatuses of Christianity and move them on to another terrain than the religious. This new terrain is faith insofar as it is the essence of Man-in-person and, in contrast to belief, assures us that we are 'in-Man' rather than 'in-Reason' or 'in-God'. A generic theology differentiates itself from philosophical theology in terms of cause, style, and effects. It is the *transformation* of the philosophical under the condition of its ultimate determination by the Man (of) faith. This must not be confused with secularization: religions and beliefs are, together, fluid and worldly, conforming to a variable yet uncertain geometry, with secularization being only one historical and worldly version.

The generic is, of course, as the example of Feuerbach shows, habitually understood as philosophical – Hegelian or para-Hegelian – and apt to be integrated under the authority of the Whole or All. But we will discern a specific structure of the generic plane, relative to Man (of) faith rather than to philosophy. The supposed 'return' taken by Feuerbach is a false one: it remains bound to a sensible-material man, which is transcendent in every way, pertaining only to a way of philosophical thought via a reversal of Hegelianism. Philosophy and theology thus re-united must be vanquished at the site of their object, Man, as well as upon the terrain of their thought, humanism and anthropology. Through the immemorial and foundational confusion that traces the outline of God in man after, first of all, tracing man in God – a profound reversal of the image of God in the human – we are 'bound' to religion. God has

His perfections, attributes, and properties, but what purpose does Feuerbach's treatment of them in terms of an alienated reflection of man and subsequent return to their supposed human origin serve? The contribution of Christianity can be found elsewhere than in this play of reflections and must not be confused with the specular character of religions.

There are, then, at least two possible interpretations of the generic: the first is philosophical, with diverse anthropological, materialist, or logical-mathematical variants; the second is non-philosophical or 'radical'. The first sense of the generic can be understood, from the outset, in the sense employed in pharmaceuticals and the sciences, where certain properties assume a universal yet not explicitly totalizing extension as discrete individuals. This is done either to replace specific or technical names, particularly with respect to a medicine (like a 'label' or commercial name – that is, a *generic* name for a drug) or, in the case of science, to redistribute them throughout a number of other disciplines. The generic founds, then, a certain univocity, without forming an explicit totality, being extended throughout a number of disciplines and fields. Understood in this manner, the generic offers a kind of 'mid-' or 'weak' philosophy, with a low profile, standing between the extremes of the One, on one side, and the Being of beings, on the other. But such generic terms offer only material for other disciplines and fields to employ for their own purposes. Without drawing all the consequences from this claim, we see nevertheless that individual things can be stripped of every 'elevated', 'spiritual', or 'ideal' predicate and brought back to a certain banality that renders their specific use as 'labels' or 'names' inoperative within particular fields. What interests us about the generic, in this first sense, is precisely its 'anti-commercial' potential as well as its universal range, without a specular double, illusion, or deception, as well as lacking any surplus value. In the end, we value the anti-capitalist destiny of the generic. But the generic remains a sub-concept, almost as inadequate for thinking Man-in-person as Feuerbach's naturalist and materialist notion.

We abandon the middle and sub-philosophical virtues of the old generic style, that is, the 'ordinary' character of this ordinary. But we do so on the sole condition of radicalizing it. This forms the second sense of the generic. A radicalization of the generic is achieved by adding another real and *a priori* condition: Man-in-person. Thus radicalized, the generic contains a mutation of the milieu – a kind of *middle unilaterality* – that is not only adapted to Man and faith but also detached or 'separated' from the theologico-philosophical order that is foreclosed to faith. This 'middle form' could be completely adapted to faith at the same time as leaving the global and the Whole or All in the hands of philosophy, which would remain implicitly in the background. But the Man (of) faith precisely radicalizes this model and manages to tear faith from the authority of the Whole and Unity. The individual nature of faith is a decision or, more precisely – in order to distance this conception of faith from Kierkegaard this time – a Decided-without-decision or even an Undecided-without-indecision that is strictly human, nothing but human. The 'middle form' manages to separate the individual from animal and rational properties, as though extracting the Man (of) faith from the entire context of predicates, humanity, history, nation, social class, and subjectivity of the subject. The 'faithful' (the only adjective admissible for faith that we will carefully distinguish from philosophical belief, which is not faithful) individual is, however, always accompanied by a very special religious structure. We no longer call this the religious – adjective for 'religion' – but rather the 'non-religious'. This sphere or this instance is universally relevant and maintains itself in the cause in-the-last-instance of being-faithful. The religious, as an adjectival, qualifying, and generic term, is thus rendered inoperative, in its usual sense, by the introduction of the Man (of) faith.

This is a special operation, lacking any synthesis. It brings a proper or singular name, without extension or comprehension, that is also empty of all predicates – not at all, however, like a common name or label in the first sense of the term 'generic' – *and* a sphere of universality together. This association is determined by identification. Rather than impose names, such an identification determines them as individual or *One(-All)*. Why put the '-All' in parenthesis? Does this not suppress the All, even diminish or reduce it, without weakening it? The reason for such a parenthesis is due to the One-in-One – an axiomatic formulation of the Real or Man-in-person – subsisting or insisting in philosophy, not as divided or doubled, but simple. Philosophy otherwise twists and turns upon within itself in a ceaseless paroxysm of thought. There is no One that might not be included in the All, thereby recovering and dividing itself, doubling the one in the other. Only a One that insists 'in'-One (One-in-One or One-in-person) can remain One and undivided, even if there is an All. The generic is a completely different logic to the philosophical one and differs partially from the logic of mathematics. If the generic needs a logic, then it is a real or transcendental, not simply a formal, one.

The most complete axiomatic formulation is, therefore, One = One-in-One = Uni–versal. There is clearly a leap, albeit only apparent, from One-in-One to Uni–versal – that is, from the radical individual to the generic individual. How can the individual be generic or universal, if it is at the same time free from the authority of philosophy? This question arises from the fact that the One-in-One has yet to be thought sufficiently insofar as without-All. The One is separated (from) the All – that is, separated without relation to or division from it. The radical immanence of the Lived-in-person makes the One-in-One as One(-Other than, not Other-of) possible, without contradiction. *We* call 'unilaterality' this structure of the One(-Other-than) that is simple or simplified, that is, without any mixture between the One-in-One and the Other. This also applies to the effects of simplification or non-sufficiency that the One brings upon the All as One(-All) and, thereby, forces philosophical thought. The One-in-One contains the 'non' of the 'non-philosophical' or a simplified philosophical approach, forced to abandon its duplicity. This is the secret of faith and the uni–versality of non-theological thought.

The radicalization of the generic allows us to understand that the generic style is the most radical mid-place or ordinary and, further, that the mid-place is a uniplace or unilateral place. The thought of the One-in-One can no longer be itself a reflected-reflexive position or an auto-position: the generic axiom is free from the vicious philosophical circle. Thanks to the totalizing and unifying ambitions of philosophy, we live with the idea that this 'mediocre' milieu or middle 'ordinary' is flanked by two supposedly extraordinary and philosophically interesting transcendences: the first moves towards the One-Being or Absolute and the second towards particular beings or objects. Both aspire towards the 'in itself'. But the problem for the generic style is acquiring human autonomy – without filling this with Being or being, totality or Idea, sensible-material or individuals supposed to be 'in themselves' – in order thus to give rise to a new experience of thought as well as a new, radical practice of ordinary language. The factor = x, which is capable of producing such effects, cannot be merely a supplement to the absolute or totality; the 'supplement' is itself generic. We call precisely the generic radical, not absolute, and *a priori* rather than in itself. This is Man-in-person. In order to transform philosophical means and virtues into the generic – that is, make them serviceable as simplified and non-duplicated material – the generic must not be denied at the very moment they are undergoing a transformation but must, instead, be delineated from the conscious-form, reflexion-form, or totality-form that is so characteristic of philosophical circularity. The major concept or dominant moment for philosophy is the One. But this is reflected in diverse degrees, like One-All, One-*of*-One, or meta-One. This means that the solution to the problem of the generic involves posing the One *without* the duplicity of the One-All and reduced, instead, to One(-All), thus depriving the philosophical One of even a reflected privation of this One-All. Man is the uni–versal *a priori* for phenomena of belief and thought – that is, the form of the world – insofar as One-in-One but also Other-than …

This subtraction of the One-in-One from the One-All, which *prima facie* appears to be accomplished through an abstraction or withdrawal, cannot be an operation performed by an agent or subject *ex machina*; rather, it arises from an immanence without substance, form, or property that is unique to the One-in-One. The double negation that philosophy poses in the One-All, like the Hegelian dialectic, is replaced with a simple 'non' or 'Other-than …' that is set within the One-in-One through a radical or positive subtraction that separates this One from the All, without ever being the object of an operation, like separation or negation. This is a positive 'Non' – real or immanent – that lacks the duplicity of positivity, that is, without the Non-of-the-Non; it is an Other, in the end, that is really without the Other-of-the-Other. The One, given as separated, hurls the absolute All – that is, in and for itself, divided and duplicated – back into a chimerical existence. Whatever instance may be marked and labelled *philosophically* as the One or Unity, that is, according to the strictures of Being or the Other, must be now un-marked. But this un-marking must, importantly, not be done twice – that is, the un-marking of the marked – as in philosophical discourse, giving thus only the appearance of un-marking; rather, it must be done once-each-time, according to radical immanence. In this way the Real, the Lived-person, is performed in a positive way as an unmarked-without-unmarking, which explains the non-sufficiency and function of this 'negative' condition underpinning the generic as well as making clear the status of the generic as an *a priori* material form for theologico-philosophical discourse. The generic possesses the virtues of a procedure or operation that productively invests itself in diverse fields without the cumbersome machinery of philosophical formalism and method. The ordinary style of the generic can be thus delivered from the claims and 'prestige' of philosophy, while still using some philosophical characteristics and operations.

The confession of faith and theological duplicity

How to think faith and religion, if neither is the object of the other? How to conceive them together without linking or binding both terms in yet another synthesis? Could this be done with a certain kind of affinity, but without co-belonging? From such questions arise a new understanding of religion that is no longer theological and authoritarian by means of concepts, great events, and dogmas, assuming thereby a triple *deus ex machina* – machine of the Church, machine of God, and machine of Philosophy – but, instead, within the limits of the human and determined on the sole basis of the Man (of) faith. The latter forms the basis for this new understanding. But it is posed-without-position or posed in terms of an axiomatic content. Knowing how to draw the effects that decline from this position suffices for this new understanding. The 'Man (of) faith' is no longer a concept, with a subject and predicates; rather, it is an indefinable or indemonstrable term. Opposite faith *ex machina* stands the axiom *fides ex homine*. If Man-in-person confesses a primacy of faith insofar as this confession lacks any object of belief – that is, a faith that is indefinable in philosophical or theological terms –, then such a confession must produce its own formulae from religious words. But such words must be emptied of any phenomena that are supposed sufficient and testify in their way to the 'freedom of the Christian'. Man-in-person proceeds by axioms that are non-reflected or non-positional decisions (of) self – they employ the non-place of philosophy, if not its 'middle' use. This needs to be a special conception of the *a priori* that is neither substantial nor formal; it must be materi*a*l, rather than materi*e*l, form*a*l, not form*e*l, *for* philosophy and theology, manifesting itself through a simplified form that differs from their initially duplicitous nature.

The central point for both theology and, from a more empirical perspective, religion is an operation of duplication. They share this in common with philosophy, but with some nuances that are irrelevant to our current purposes. Such operations amount to a 'demonstration' or at the very least an argument (or 'proof') for the existence of God. The express or stated proofs for the existence of God are useless insofar as a redoubling of bad conscience or *resentiment*. They are, in any case, phenomena resulting from duplicity and belief, not the work of faith. No more than religions or theology, the existence of God does not need to be proven; there is a God, like there is religion, although neither is *real*. Even scepticism and atheism, under their philosophical form, often form an integral part of the inner life of religion. But they cannot determine faith as a Lived material and a formal *a priori*. On the contrary, faith is a Truth-without-truth, which makes possible an effect of truth that is inseparable from it – even if faith itself remains foreclosed to atheism, scepticism, and, furthermore, to 'truths' and religious beliefs. This is the condition for faith to work with such beliefs. The operation of faith is an immanent work.

Faith and dualyzation of belief

Man is, above all, not a believing animal, as Feuerbach implies in the purest theological-philosophical tradition. Man only becomes a believer through an alienation from the religious. Belief possesses or is possessed; faith, however, is neither acquired nor possessed. Faith is neither innate nor an originary acquisition but declines from the *a priori* real, that is, material and formal. Faith is inalienable, even if the veil of religion covers it. Man as a believing animal is a symptom of the longest running error, turning Man into a being of the world that is destined to an infinite vertigo. If vertigo is the horror of the void, God alone can stabilize and bind us to the world. This experience is the responsibility of God, who has not found a more effective means to bind us to Him than vertigo and horror. This is, perhaps, the only true function of God as Grand Corruptor: to bind us, body and soul, to the world. But there is no interval between Man – that is, there is no distance, no movement 'to Man', only an immediate 'in-Man' – wherein a perfection, reason, or an attribute can lodge itself. If Man is, indeed, an animal, then the ascription 'rational' follows, too. But Man is neither animal nor rational – all such predicates happen to him afterwards. Deprived of predicates, and, consequently, lacking any subject, Man is only in-Man, rather than in-animal or in-reason. Faith is without-object as much as without-subject for the same reason. It cannot arise as part of a process of consciousness or religion, even if this follows in the wake of the non-religious. Faith is the impalpable substance or human ether before being an object or subject of belief; it does not and cannot dissolve itself in the world.

The fundamental axiom of non-theology is that faith and belief, far from being mixed together and confused, form a unilateral duality. They must be thought together each time, *as faith, not belief, only belief as faith in-the-last-instance*, contrary to the habit of philosophy.

There is, perhaps, too much belief! What matters is subjecting belief to the test of faith. Faith is immanent, while belief participates in this immanence. But on this view, belief is thus transformed into 'non-belief', turning against its religious exteriority. Belief is thus Other than 'itself' – it could even be called 'generic belief'. Faith is unique or univocal for all belief, but belief is double – an appearance that must be understood as such unilaterally, rather than as a duality of beliefs.

Faith is 'in-faith' or 'in-person' and is not definable in terms of belief. But this does not mean that faith is the absolute absence of belief. This would be an abstraction. Faith is rather a real or radical absence of belief, as we have said, thus also a 'non-belief' rather than an absolute rejection of any phenomena of belief. What does this mean? The 'non' of non-belief is the ingredient of faith that determines belief and binds it to a transcendent religious form (one is tempted to say 'religionals'). Faith 'does-not-*believe*' in belief rather than faith; it believes in the non-existence of belief. The primacy of faith uses belief precisely through unilateralization, inversion, and 'turning against', that is, for itself, against religious forms. Faith does not divide belief but rather dualyzes or separates it, not from itself but from the 'Identity of faith' that determines it. The dualyzation of belief by faith does not distinguish between two types of belief but rather effectuates a mutation upon belief that separates without dividing it. Being the Real of Man, faith is, in effect, without-relation. Belief that is supposed to be isolated in its philosophical element is relation. Consequently, non-belief is, in essence, without-relation, and so remains a non-relation, whereby the 'non' expresses the without-relation of faith.

Faith and belief are not two psychic or conscious attitudes in themselves, totally separate and without communication, or even communicating to one another within a mixture of philosophical styles. If there were two reciprocally heterogeneous and, therefore, 'mixable' attitudes, more or less 'enduring', then faith would fall back into an interiority explored from St Augustin to Kierkegaard. Likewise, belief that is supposed to be solely or absolutely autonomous in the same way would consequently become once again an ecstatic grasping for an object, whereas generic or ordinary belief possesses only a relative autonomy to the radicality of faith in which it participates. They are not two things, divided and then (possibly) mixed; the essence of faith is not belief or affected by belief; it is its own solitude. Belief is, conversely, not affected by faith, but – and this is completely different – relates without-relation to faith or non-belief. This excludes religious belief as much as the absolute absence of any belief (atheism).

Faith marks an adhesion neither to God and His intentions of love – this would be an 'evident (or positive) belief' – nor to itself in a pure intention towards something, without an intended object (i.e. an empty intentionality), turning forever in the wind, as if the intentional relation were fulfilled by a rigorous empty- or void-relation, like contemporary philosophers, fearful of such positivity, often maintain. This is the schema of faith understood as transcendence – that is, as belief or non-belief, as a faithful response or an atheism (amply filled with either itself or the negation of God), even an intention that is, in one way or another, saturated by God (Marion and Levinas), whether present or absent, revealed or well hidden. It is even doubtful that faith is *fides qua creditur*, that is, a faith leading to and sustaining belief. There are too many theologians on the hunt for beneficence (e.g. the Good, the Beautiful), not enough seek poverty and nudity. Faith cannot be defined in phenomenological terms, that is, as a relation to the world or an intentionality, variously understood, interpreted, and modified. It undoes the narcissism of the transcendental consciousness (Husserl) and transcendence, which, in the best possible case, founds a phenomenology, that is, provides a Logos. But faith has priority over the Logos; it gives the Logos in a radically reduced unilateral manner, rather than as an intentional correlate. It has this priority, not insofar as an intentionality but insofar as it sub-tends Man; that is, it is the 'real-ation' of its own essence, which sub-tends, as a dimension of pure futurality, on the basis that this can establish something like an intentionality. Faith can appear to our contemporaries as the 'last chance' for phenomenology and the adventures and intrigues of transcendence, presenting a modified understanding of presence that is neutralized with respect to the object or marking its absence, even its failure sometimes – an act without foresight but also the most minimal attestation. The nature of this faith is futurality or messianity; it is not a response to an announcement or a call, like *kerygma*, but rather God manifesting faith via the creation or the transcendence of grace. In any case, Man appears in the world under the clandestine form of faith. What would clandestine faith look like, that is, a faith untouched by the philosopher's intention *ex machina*, who would take hold of it once again only to put it back into the service of philosophy and the world that the faithful would be bound to transform? Contrary to bad philosophical conscience, faith does have a 'correlate'. But this correlate has nothing at all to do with a present/absent object, since the correlate of faith is the world insofar as given *a priori* or as material. Faith is an *a priori* material that gives the world in a uni-originary manner, that is, otherwise than originary, which is nothing other than the originary faith of phenomenologists and the philosophers of ordinary language. This faith cannot but flee from itself. It is the *a priori* material that presents to us an homo-ontology and homousia but reduced or non-hallucinatory. Philosophy confuses the sub-donation of faith with the donation of an absence as well as the sub-tending to the world with a flight before the presence of the world. But Man scarcely flees presence or representation; rather, Man has an *a priori* access to them for the first and last time. As ever, philosophical constructions commit a sin by their abstraction or construction upon already ruined empirical bases. Philosophers of Being – the sense, truth, location, even the non-presence and *aporia* of Being – mark still an effort undertaken in order to convey and distribute the most immanent faith. This is done almost always in terms of flight, retreat, subtraction, absence, lack, the step back (Heidegger), reserve – in short, a *worldly* clandestine character. But we think that faith and the grace given to it must be inverted. Under the condition of the primacy of Man, understood to be foreclosed to faith and constituted by belief, faith sub-tends as grace, with one or the other destined for the world.

Faith, fidelity, and grace

There is no originary continuity between faith and the belief-world; even generic belief does not offer a mediation, only a unilateral instrument or a proper act of faith, namely a non-act. This is the generic sense of non-theology. Faith is not, therefore, an abrogated or contracted belief, like certain pietists; it is, in essence, not objective, only then to be interiorized or diminished. The radicality of the Lived-in-Person does not come under the form of consciousness, subjectivity, or a life, along with diverse modalities of reception and belief, but rather in a quasi-materiality, structured wholly in accordance with immanence. Faith is thus empty 'of' belief in a way that is empty (of) the void-of-belief itself or the other-than-belief, too. The radical individual, deprived of any predicates and relations, opposes itself to the religious or existential subject of philosophical and theological beliefs. Faith is not here a subjective and pietist experience, that is, individual and un-sayable; it is not an interiority opposed to the transcendence of religion. Faith is certainly not a 'faith in man', like Christian humanism, but faith 'in-Man' – that is, faith as a human posture, other than via predicates. Man is not the subject of faith but rather the real content of it.

A *doxa* is a nest of suppositions and ambiguities – it is a belief that 'holds true'. This is, when correctly understood, only belief lacking fidelity. Something that 'holds' in this way is an objectifying or ecstatic comportment, according to the rigour of a conscious intention seizing and then appropriating an object of truth or something liable to be true, perhaps, in a dialectical way. Regardless of the finesse and delicacy of such a grasp, it nevertheless pushes the object into the world in a way that confuses the True-without-truth with the truth. There is, in addition, another possible definition that proceeds by way of subtraction this time. This possesses 'a certitude without proof' – this absence of proof takes us back towards truth understood in the first sense, that is, to take 'for' true. The passible truth or reality is a certitude performed in a modality of the intentional subject, always as transcendence and representation. Faith is not a belief, like an object, that is, an ecstatic, transcendent act. By declaring faith to be radically human, we do not exceed Man through yet another modality or predicate, introducing yet another variation; on the contrary, faith introduces a post-dicate or new immanent work for Man precisely through the way this determines the world. Faith neither takes an object = x for truth – that is, something liable to or admitting truth – nor makes truth an attribute or predicate of a thing; rather, faith 'takes' *the True for itself, even if it is non-sufficient to itself.* The True of the Real is not a *product* of truth or reality, like a mark or label; rather, it is a performed hypothesis or a lived in-immanence, not a speculative hypothesis or mere possibility that is supposed to be self-founded. The True of the Real is called a posture that engages Man as in-Man, rather than a position in the world or a pre-determined thought, like philosophy. Faith is humanly sufficient, religiously insufficient;

belief is humanly alienating, religiously sufficient. Faith, along with the ingredient of generic belief, determines or clones beliefs by withdrawing the non-religious from the fabric of religion. For Man, there is faith; for the faithful subject, there is the struggle with belief and the fidelity of their works performed through this struggle.

There are precisely two ways to grant consistency to an act of faith: either by adding an object of the world to faith or by recognizing the identity of an actual messianic coming in faith. The latter is the sole form of human consistency, that is, not worldly, but can nevertheless transform the form-world. The messianity of faith is not an object. Even an object yet to come remains an object already in the past. Faith is empty of world-belief, certainly, but resists being faith *in (or of) nothing* (nihilism); rather, it is in-faith or *fidelity* – that is, a posture of fidelity 'in' the Last-Instance or 'in' Last Things. This fidelity 'in' Identity is an empty intention, that is, unilateral or Other than …. It comes directly to the subject (the identity of a clonage) in a non-ecstatic manner but comes to the world in an indirect or ecstatic manner, if the world is given in an illusionary doubling or duplicity (like Hegel). The characteristics and traits used so far to define faith signal a grace that comes from No Part, rendering unnecessary any attribution to a Creator and Sovereign Being or a religious subject – both necessary for alienation.

Belief as unilateral paradox

One doubts whether faith without-relation will manage to preserve a rather curious non-relation to the relations of a discourse that it determines and to which it will refer as to an object or world. But such a faith does not intend to do this and, furthermore, cannot do so. Whence follows the axiom that replaces the usual discourse of the theological Word and puts to flight the paradoxes of belief (along with their dialectical form), setting in their place a much simpler form. In any case, the paradox, along with its dissolution, stands somewhere between religion, understood in terms of an ecstatic belief in Man or faith as object, and faith, which refuses such objectification or ecstatic grasp (see above). The paradox is only unilateral and only has value as the Word insofar as this expresses the religious and philosophical point of view.

Belief and faith are often confused in religions – it is even their principle. From this follows the renewal of the very paradoxes that theologians and priests employ in order to bewitch and beguile 'believers' and thereby turn them away from the path of fidelity. In contrast, faith is simple: it is a response-without-question. Faith remains silent for as long as we do not attempt to say it. But faith becomes paradoxical as soon as there is a need to say it, although without any supposed impossible utterance; indeed, there is a sense in which faith must always be said insofar as we constrain ourselves by faith or demand beliefs and religions from it. Yet when we think according to faith, paradoxes arise only when such a thought starts to take a turn towards faith as though towards a referent (i.e. an object) – that is, according to beliefs, not faith, as we so often imagine. Such paradoxes have nothing at all to do with the Absolute, like Hegel, or the dialectic between the real and language, like Kierkegaard. On the contrary, thought and discourse are, in non-theology, determined in-the-last-instance by faith, which is completely foreclosed to them both and cannot be mixed dialectically with it. The transcendent paradoxes that beset theology and religion are found not in faith or language but in their mixture. They become unilateral and immanent, thereby ceasing to be resolved into such a dialectical reversibility, however, when Man-in-Man, understood as Other-than … world, language, thought, and so on, determines or clones a faithful subject, starting from their material. Faith is, then, unintelligible in terms of philosophy, but no longer a problem for the faithful. Yet this must nevertheless be said and, indeed, needs to be said with the help of philosophy and theology. Insofar as indefinable and un-demonstrable, faith supports a certain kind of axiom. As inexplicable, even according to religious explanations, and, therefore, heretical, arguments can nevertheless be formed on this subject. Being non-existent in religion or history, faith does not, however, cease to act upon them. Faith haunts the world, giving itself 'to' but without alienating itself 'in' the world. Faith is *for* the world, without being representational; it is open to the world, without ecstasis. Non-subjective, faith holds itself firm to the immanent lived – that is most immanent to Man, with every fibre. Seemingly the most immaterial, faith has the consistency of a transparent and ideal materiality. As ultimate human substance, faith is not a mental object (for thought) but a phenomena through and through. Every paradox arises for the first time from a poor reversible conjugation of faith and language. But they arise again for a second time from the unilateral unition of faith and cloning in religious language.

When faith is recognized as Real-in-Person, without being a thing in itself, but rather as an *a priori* form *for* philosophy and theology – that is, a non-belief that suspends them in their sufficiency and gives them back in this way, then dialectical paradox is thereby dissolved, without disappearing altogether, No one 'has' or 'is' faith; rather, faith is the identity (of) the person in the sense of the 'in-person' of Man; it is never an attribute or supplement that could be ascribed to an entity, rational or not. We could parody the mystic and say: 'faith is without why' (Angelus Silesius). But this does not mean at all that faith *believes* because it is absurd (*credo quia absurdum*) or even paradoxical. On the contrary, nothing is less absurd than being a Man (of) faith who does not believe in such and such historico-worldly content, dogma, doctrine, symbol, or religious person. If there is, indeed, a paradox, then this does not result from faith but from thought according to faith.

We will continue to follow in the wake left by the paradoxes of religion – that is, the fractal line of unilateral duality or the unshared share that returns to identifications – that form the basis for the belief-world and thereby *in-verts* them. The dialectical paradox is made immanent and unilateral, without, importantly, being completely effaced. It must be regarded from each side of the unilateral duality in a way that maintains the primacy of human faith over the religious, which thereby includes the in-immanence in the human, as though radical faith cut loose a religion-fiction that would eventually give rise to a theo-fiction made from the remnants of theology and the history of religion. The terms of fiction clearly do not send us back into the imaginary, make-believe, or fairy tale; rather, such a fiction is the most extreme form of paradox, arriving after it has been torn from the world and transformed into a non-religious paradox.

Faith as *a priori* posture

The efforts of Feuerbach come to mind – that is, the humanist and sensible or material reduction of religious transcendence from divine predicates to the generic individual. But what we propose does not directly concern such efforts. Man-in-Person, as more immanent to me than myself, when understood as a subject, constitutes the Real of religion, but, importantly, not in an anthropological and material-sensible manner. This is the generic individual, radicalized and separated, in essence, from all worldly content – psychological as much as mystical and theological. Understood as Real-in-Person, faith is not a thing in itself but an *a priori* that is identically formal *and* material *for* philosophy and theology; it is a non-belief that at once gives them and suspends their supposed sufficiency. Generic faith – that is, a non-philosophical fidelity – is structured in a way that could be called a posture. If a position is doctrinal, then posture is properly or most radically human but furnished with a simple alterity or otherness in a unilateral manner; and, further, if a position is totalizing by vocation, posture is only universal, without being totalizing in the same way a religion or Catholic theology, which is too quickly philosophical or under the authority of Unity, can form a totality. Faith is not a unity, integrating a multiplicity into a union. It is an identity with a simple Other-than … side or aspect and is, therefore, more originary than philosophical belief. Faith is uni-originary, while philosophy is proto-originary – this makes the difference between grace and metaphysical volition.

The foregoing explains how a non-religious usage of religion, outside its theoretical and institutional pomp, may be possible. Why a non-theological use of theology? Within a generic thought of faith stands the radical presupposition of the non-religious, not religion (this presupposition would amount to an essence of religion). The non-religious is foreign or foreclosed to religion. Religion does not find the inscrutable source of its origin here but rather the cause of its eventual transformation from an hallucinatory religion into a non-religious phenomenon. What is most real offers itself as a secret – it only ever insists and remains to be discovered (or un-covered). But this most real is, at the same time, over-determined through the appearance of religious beliefs, owing precisely to its pure identity, without existence, and the way the real distinguishes itself from such appearances in principle. Once the unilateral duality of faith and religions is admitted, more than their difference, then the contingency of their worldly expressions and works can be posed.

Profess or confess faith?

This universal sphere, determined by Man, starting from religious symptom, resembles a predicate, but without actually being one, and looks like a relation, while being only a non-relation. Whence the ever-present possibility of the philosophical and theological capture of the faithful Man for the benefit of belief. But the reduction of the religious by non-religious faith helps avoid the Charybdis and Scylla of modernity, namely the dogma and practice of infallibility that maintains the consistency of the Church (and churches) as well as the narcissistic proclamation of opinions that characterize the ideological, financial, and sometimes sexual exploitation of humans by cults, something churches remain too complacent about. The non-religious plane demands the renunciation of any and every religious ambition towards totalitarian – sometimes criminal – subjection of humans as well as the narcissistic chatter that some ceaselessly propound, casting their miserable opinions to all winds. Nevertheless, the absurd and impossible exclusion of religions must be avoided. In virtue of the non-sufficiency of fidelity, reference must be made to them, but only in an occasional manner, like our reference to Christianity, and, of course, other religions. A radicalized human is the *a priori* 'form' and 'matter' for a thought that deduces itself occasionally from religion and theology, without being a part of them, and, therefore, relevant for Man outside the 'false universal' that is gathered together in various ways under the modern name of the 'subject' that dissimulates absolute Subjectivity. The distinction between generic Man and the subject is 'without return' – that is, unilateral – and permits the use of religion and the history of theology, without becoming a believer, and confess faith, without being confessional. The unilateral distinction means that the subject derives from Man, without, importantly, exhausting its content.

A new possible confusion arises: the proclamation or profession of faith is, perhaps, a Christian act that is always a *pro*-clamation or *pro*-fession 'in the eyes of the world' that is left to be gathered up or interpreted according to the wisdom of belief – a re-vindication and soon, perhaps, martyrdom – but this is done *in place of confessing for the World* – that is, in order to transform such confession into a work of salvation. If God has, indeed, bungled creation, why would believers not also more or less botch salvation? Un-covert yourselves! – this is an 'order-word' to say in the secret, hidden depths of one's heart. This must be done, not like a de-conversion or de-construction, like a satanic contrary of conversion, but rather like a *uni–version* of faith *for* the World and religion. This is, doubtless, the single most coherent way to 'in-vert' religions and their universal call to conversion.

The identity-in-the-last-instance of faith and religion

The generic problematic does not concern the philosophical constants of rupture and re-unification. *There is a unity, certainly, but this unity is not real.* There is no question here of healing historico-religious cuts and scissions – that is, any kind of schism or split that motivates the intense theological activity of patching and 'suturing'. The febrile desire for unity and ecumenical consensus – that is, all that concerns religions that feel one step behind life and, more broadly, out-of-step with history – is not a generic affect. An heretical sensibility concerns, indeed, the forces of rupture, schism, break, and so forth but, far from appealing to unity, engages with them, instead, insofar as immediate derivatives of an Identity that accompany this like an effect of a force, namely, the force of a duality or an irreducible dualyzation. *This Identity is real, without existing.* The generic presents itself as an hypo-thesis, that is, a position, but made supple by not being an auto-position. It is a uni-thesis, without syn-thesis. The generic undoes classical and contemporary philosophical representation through the association of an aspect of faith and the non-religious in a way that means that the generic and the philosophical do not communicate with or participate in one another in any kind of exchange; they are irreducible to one another in-the-last-instance.

In order to better guarantee the fusion of the Man (of) faith and religion in a non-historical practice of salvation, the duality of faith and religion will need to be re-affirmed from the perspective of their 'complementarity' – that is, their real fusion, without *con*-fusion. But this complementarity is not really complementary, since this rests upon their *unilateral* duality. A unilateral duality can, indeed, accommodate a unity. But such a unity is not posed in an immanent way in a duality. A unilateral duality only tolerates a unilateral unity or unilateral appearance. Unity only really occurs by supplementing a duality. Unilateral duality is, indeed, not without unity. But such a unity does not form part of a system that draws together a duality or pair; instead, this unity is brought together without thickness or density at a single, non-reflected, and transcendental level that supplements the duality or pair, without, importantly, suppressing or overcoming (like Hegel – *Aufhebung*) them. This is a unilateral supplementarity or complementarity. The complementarity of faith and the religious constitutes a unilateral style, not exactly physico-quantic. The duality of faith and the religious is thus safeguarded at the same time as reduced to an aspect of faith (i.e. determining essence) and the non-religious (i.e. the existence of faith) by means of a non-relation – that is, the Man (of) faith.

The category of the non-religious Christian

A name must be set within the generic order or regime that serves to nominate the emergence of this new generic 'posture' rather than a philosophico-theological one. The generic Christian will therefore be considered as (1) a real object, that is, a determining cause of the non-relation or the relation-without-support to religions, and Christ understood not as religious object of faith but as Man (of) faith, whom we try to 'imitate'; the generic Christian indicates (2) the employment of a religion that rejects the ethnic and mythological soil from which Christ draws His references, like, for example, the Judaic tradition. The generic gives rise to (3) a discourse that forms the kind of decision we have already used – that is, symbols or axioms of faith – but ones that are real this time and called 'non-religious'; the generic Christian generates (4) a concept of the religious that is 'non-religious' – a post-dicate (as opposed to pre-dicate) that adds nothing to the real of faith and merits, therefore, being called a religious transcendental.

Faith, religion, and the non-religious are thus distributed according to unilateral relations. They cannot be redistributed and their content cannot be transformed without denying this distribution and calling it into question. They are special relations that sometimes resemble dogmas but have, in fact, little, if anything, to do with them, except as symptoms that help elaborate the category of the 'non-religious'. Such affirmations will be taken up in axioms, without seeking to prove (or demonstrate) them: *there is a (non-)religious or belief, but neither the (non-)religious nor belief is real. The religious is not real.* What (is) real is Man and only Man (not the subject) – that is, faith, not belief. The religious does not determine Man-in-Person. It is the reverse: Man determines the religious, without any reciprocal determination. We 'believe' in the religious, not within the limits of religions but within the bounds of the radical human – it is the religious-without-religion.

The non-religious is not, therefore, the absolute absence or negation of religion *in toto* but rather a transcendental neutralization or suspension of their sufficiency. Even if the non-religious is not, in this strong sense, the Real and lacks any power to determine it, there remains nevertheless the (non-)religious – sometimes the only apparent form in the World and history. The structures and institutions of religions – that is, the concepts, dogmas, beliefs, historical events, and the hierarchical and socio-political structures of the churches – form the conditions for the existence and exercise of faith in the world. But this is not faith as such. This forms the radical presupposition for such structures and makes their operation possible. The churches and their religions reach their aspirations, even apotheosis, in the process of globalization, forming themselves on the basis of belonging and upon affirmations of cultural identity. They have become the means for geo-political domination, sharing spheres of influence in a global struggle.

But what does this now mean? Under what axiomatic form 'is there' the religious? The religious is clearly no longer an empirical or historical constant, since there are many other things in the world. The 'there is' is an *effect of not being, for religion, the Real.* This particular understanding of the *'there is'* indicates precisely what is *not* the Man (of) faith but nevertheless determined by him, starting from religious material; in other words, the *'there is'* names the non-religious that accompanies the Man (of) faith and forms the world for the subject. This neutralization of religious signifies that the non-religious is the religion that is now determined by the Man (of) faith; it is what remains of its complexity when it has passed into and made a *tabula rasa, without overcoming or suppressing it.* The non-religious is ideal, like a surface or very fine film, that accompanies Man, without having any thickness or density reflected and duplicated through the philosophico-theological religious. It is a universal and sterile Idea that insists; it is an un-attributed attribute of Man – a post-dicate that affects the non-religious; it is the sterile correlate of the (unilateral duality of) faith. The non-religious insists rather than exists – existence belongs to religions. The religious has a way of being – *a way of there is*, rather, or sterility – that can only be formulated, if not determined, through the duplicity of theology and its structures, that is, from its double nature. Such a subtraction is made, in reality, through a forced 'bracketing' or suspension of religious sufficiency. What remains after this subtraction is effectively only Man, and such a formulation is *brought about* as an objective appearance through the axiom that makes this power less *relationnel* than *unilationnel*. What is thus brought about by faith, without being related, is a philosophical sense, but lacking any reflected concept; in short, it is a theology without Logos and, therefore, without dogma – a transcendence without transcending, a creation without creator, a spiritual body without Church, a liturgy without order.

There is, therefore, a knowledge that follows from faith, beyond the lived – precisely a belief. The Man (of) faith is foreclosed to the theologian, as a mixed being, but must make use of theology on condition of simplifying it, first of all, through a doubling that obtains a theologically sterile dimension or surface that is neither meta- nor *epekeina*-physical – an indivisible shaft or wave, without density or reflected thickness, without calculation or strategy of conquest. A transcendental theological appearance adds nothing at all to the real of faith, which itself follows by procession only from faith and emerges through the continual encounter between faith and religion. It makes the principle minimal or weak through a qualitative simplification of the theological violence – via concepts and dogmas – that draws abundantly from the mythological foundations of the religious. This process of 'making minimal' and the basis for this minimal principle is from now on salvation and life in the world, ordered according to the action of faith, understood as non-action, whence follows a minimum of thought with respect to this faith. This weakening marks the end of the transcendent and authoritarian force of dogma as well as the Church that pronounces them.

The fragile and weak force of fidelity needs an *a priori* defence. This defence consists in the works that constitute the thought of faith. There is no need to borrow or draw from already constituted philosophy. This is the benefit that results from the fragility and weakness of faith, understood as the action of a non-action. Far from being submitted to a foreign thought, like philosophy, and ordered to the structures of churches and religions, faith is accompanied, without any reciprocal participation, by a thought that has no need for philosophy. Thought determined by the generic has an 'objective' transcendental appearance, drawn from religion as its occasion. Any knowledge determined by faith and any statements that are transformed by dogmas and theological concepts demonstrate as far as possible the status of their truth. This is, then, a distribution of thought that has been lifted out from theology alone and set out, in an equitable manner, upon the basis of the Last-Instance throughout all generic activities. The faith of the 'simple' is not itself a thought. Does this, however, determine one as against the God of the philosophers and the scientists? Not at all – the call of the Man (of) faith, that is, the force that is employed to impose a new life upon beliefs, is very far from the appeal of the philosophers, and, as if through a parry or counter-blow, much closer to the scientific effort, without, importantly, being *in sensu stricto* a positive science.

During our time, where the barbarity of certain religions divides the world into the 'faithful' and the 'unfaithful', where ecumenism-without-thought and the sectarian spirit, compromise and fundamentalism, become independent forces in a continual struggle with one another, splitting the sphere of religions in two, we take pleasure in applying the name 'faithful' only to those whose thoughts and acts reveal the Man (of) faith, that is, not the 'last faith' (a good slogan for a sect), but faith as last instance, which resolves such antinomies. Fidelity cannot be the 'last refuge for the faithful'; on the contrary, it is universal and available to the whole world, which, unfortunately, continues to see faith, less than the light of reason, as divisible.

The foregoing can be summarized in the following manner: (1) a religion always exists as a suppression that is exercised against human subjects or Man-as-Subjects – this is the religion-world; (2) the religious insists, like the non-religious, as a transcendental universal that applies to every phenomena in the world – it is a 'spinozist' attribute through which everything can be seen.

The Name-of-Christ as first symbol

The generic interpretation of the event of Christ makes this name the first among first names for the confession of faith. This nomination must function as a singular or proper name, if it is to retain the status of a common origin, even as far as being empty of any content or referent. If there is, indeed, an historical or theological reference, however, then this is an entirely occasional one – that is, only apparent or without reciprocal relation, adding nothing at all to the Real of the symbol that deploys such referents as material. Christianity, as religion, whether faithful or not, is a transcendental determination that adds nothing to the real of Christ or at least nothing real to Christ. The symbol 'Christ' *uni-fers rather than refers* to a new lived or experience, namely the non-religious, ever faithful, but only in-the-last-instance. This distinguishes it from the religious of religions in general, in particular Christianity. It must always be possible to say, using theological vocabulary, for example, that *Christ is in-Christ or in-Person*, or even, as some orthodox mystics proclaim: 'Jesus!', 'Jesus!'. The claim that Christ is not Christian is too easy. But the claim that only a Christ-without-Christianity, that is, a faithful rather than a believing Christ, must determine historical Christianity and lift this from the turpitude of history is much more difficult to admit and take seriously. We only use the formula Christ 'without-Christianity' in order to counter the current claim within the Church, namely, the Unity in Multiplicity and Multiplicity in Unity, according to the Greco-Papist formula. Otherwise, each man is 'once and each time' a 'Christian' subject for as long as the Name-of-Christ is taken as the first symbol according to faith.

The generic name is a proper name, human, but not a subject. It no longer carries any predicates. This name is first and empty of any and every determining predicate. It holds precisely *for* the context of predicates upon which it has ceased to be founded in order to be defined. In reality, the first or generic name cannot be defined, only accompanied by predicates (i.e. as post-dicates). The first name must, then, be an act of an axiomatic nature that is defined only indirectly by its effects. But this radicalized generic is completely different from a mathematical logic, understood in a restrictive or disciplinary sense, as well as, of course, philosophical logic. If this logic is, indeed, close to an axiomatic, then this is real and transcendental, not simply formal. If philosophy has learnt to speak in the language of concepts, then generic Man – that is, Man (of) science and Man (of) faith – speaks in axioms, modulated each time in accordance with different material. Faith no longer arises from a 'mathematical divine' of salvation or even a transcendent grace, like philosophers often describe; rather, faith is a mathematical human (science) or a faithful salvation (faith). The axiom of faith, recall, is that *the One is Uni–versal*.

In order to save faith from the influence of religions that found the world and, further, transform this into the determining cause of the religious, as transcendental, then the axiomatic process must be carefully specified, since it has many faces or aspects and is always apt to be interpreted as abstraction, extraction, separation, subtraction, or deconstruction. In a sense, faith must be able to make use of and, indeed, explain such operations. This consists, for example, in extracting the core or nucleus of faith and thereby causing it to appear outside various 'envelopes' and 'manifolds', in particular theology. But this extraction is not, however, an operation of separation(s), since faith is given along with Man as already separated before all separation – that is, as foreclosed to such an operation. Does this form, then, a new way of marking or labelling faith outside the context of the Logos? But human faith is already marked, pronounced and posed, as first without any operation of *re*-marking, although we do, indeed, seem to re-mark or re-double faith, owing to its symbolic nature, through its withdrawal from religion. But this is, importantly, determined in immanence. Does this offer a way to subtract faith from the Logos? But it is already subtracted, rather than waiting to be subtracted; the axiom is only a subtraction to the extent that it is posed starting from the discursive religious material of the religious.

What is this process that is not a separate operation yet does not act upon its object? A deeper and more profound examination of confession and the way it uses symbols is needed. But a confession of faith can already be understood not to take any position in the context of religion and philosophy, that is, to pose an action in the world, or deconstruct the sediments of theology. This confession is a posture, not a position, and manifests itself through axioms rather than concepts. Yet axioms find (1) their determining cause in Identity via the immanence of faith, without being performative – indeed, they are performative-without-performation; axioms find (2) their means of action in 'generic belief' – that is, empty and non-ecstatic; and axioms find (3) their worldly or mundane material in the theologico-philosophical field. It is from this material that axioms arise, after being transformed, and thus they bring this material along, too, but without, importantly, any relation to faith. Faith acts by a decision for generic belief, which is empty. But the void of this generic belief brings about, in a uni-lational manner, the very material it transforms. The axiom here is no longer posed by a transcendent agent *ex machina*, like a mathematician, philosopher, or theologian, or even a mixture of these persona, but rather by the Man (of) faith as subject. It is not, therefore, mathematical, logico-formal, or founded upon an internal and intuitive transcendental experience, which lacks the axiom-form in the modern sense. Rather, the axiom is real, but not intuitive, and transcendental (in the modern sense) insofar as it refers this time to the philosophically and theologically given material (this marks its uni-lational character).

The symbols of non-Christianity must be inscribed and function within this quasi-axiomatic framework. Since this framework has nothing, or very little, to do with a logico-formal axiomatic, attention will now turn towards the linguistic symbol in order to delineate and define in some way the uni-lational object and the cause of their non-relation: Christ-in-Christ or Christ-in-Person. What this name models, beyond the directly historical Jesus, is the Real (of) faith as well as a symbol that is lived in-the-last-instance in faith or 'in-faith' (in-faithfulness). The first names do not validate their objects externally, as if from outside, with the help of a definition, but rather with the occasional help of religion, especially by and from their immanence in the Real. Faith is confessed with the help of the world insofar as Other-than … the world. The problem of 'relation(s)' will be taken together with the problem of the confession of faith. But the unilateral or uni-lational symbol is without any synthesis with its cause – faith being real only by being without object(s). The status of this confession (of faith) in terms of separation (by immanence) and the absence of any object form the basis for drawing unilateral relations among religious objects, not precisely relations but uni-lations. The 'empty tomb' – the substance of faith – is uni-lational and offers a modified form or model to religion, namely the non-religious.

The work of the confession of faith

The work belonging to faith is immanent, understood as in-the-last-instance of a faithful non-act. But this non-act remains, nevertheless, an act – that is, an act of generic belief or non-belief. This non-act is distinct from what is done or performed and transforms the accomplished act into a *minima* for this relation. This holds equally for the axiom – the matrix for all work – that passes through the Word and takes works already accomplished in the world as its object. The work belonging to faith takes its force and consistency to be True by and from itself but remains deprived of the means to truth that signals the transformation of theologico-philosophical symptoms. The consistency of faith implies a radical philosophical inconsistency – that is, the foreclosure of faith to the Logos. The axiom could be understood to be the exercise of a radical inconsistency – that is, Man as the void of everything, except Man, and therefore, faithful. This marks the value of the foregoing structure, understood as a subtraction from the concept and reduced to the purely sterile presence of the (non-)religious.

A confession of faith is traditionally made in statements that have a particular form, namely as a 'symbol' or 'symbol of faith'. The symbol-form of confession and faith has not yet been elaborated sufficiently, obviated so far by public confessions, professions, or political protestation, even dialectical expressions: 'I believe ... I confess (the divinity of Christ, for example).' The term 'symbol' indicates a 'saying-by-symbols' or axioms in such a way that they are performed in-the-last-fidelity. This is only clear if the linguistic and psychoanalytic signification of this term is taken back towards its more formal usage and, further, that taken together they are returned to faith as their determinant. Far from being merely a formal material, a literal or instrumental symbol, and so on, the faithful intention, understood precisely as faith, coming from nowhere, forms the basis for Man. This empty intention animates speech devoted to and destined for the world.

With respect to the difficult yet decisive problem of *the symbol of faith*, we have already suggested that this must be treated within the framework of an axiomatics of fidelity. We pose, first of all, that the traditional symbol of faith, as understood by Christianity, is, in fact, a *profession* of belief or something done 'in the eyes of the world'. From a philosophical perspective, the traditional symbol is founded upon the inseparability of the signifying and signified and on a certain perfomativity of spoken language, even upon linguistic acts that are always transcendent. This precipitates the fall of the traditional symbol directly into the grasp of the religious. We pose, in the second place, the conversion, even the uni–version, of the symbol(s) of belief into a true symbol of faith, but under an axiomatic form this time. We understand the symbol(s) of faith in general to be a special kind of axiom and will, then, speak henceforth of 'symbols' rather than axioms.

A wholly immanent faith confesses or 'lets itself be confessed'. It is the action of the non-act of faith. This is how the religious *shows* or *manifests* itself precisely as the non-religious – the proper work of faith. There is a constant confusion between the work of belief and the specific work of faith. From this follows an insoluble antithetical relation between faith and work that arises and unfolds within the element of belief and ecstatic transcendence. If such a manifestation within the sphere of the religious, including the Christian milieu, were called the 'symbol of faith' in the generic posture as faith-in-person, which is itself the symbol that is symbolized-without-symbolization, where an accomplished operation of the logos or language no longer plays a determining role, then this would be precisely an occasional material for an immanent, non-religious faith. The confession of faith sustains an indivisible relation – a 'without-relation' – between the signifying and the signified, the utterance and the uttered, that differs from the way they 'co-belong' in religion, which precisely talks about a *profession* of faith with confession as much as faith with belief. By contrast, the confession of faith marks *an indivision between saying faith and faith itself – it is a unilateral Identity, rather than a reciprocal or reversible one*. This indivision is precisely the faith that is foreclosed to the divisions and distinctions in discourse but at the same time determines this very discourse. The determining role of faith arises precisely from this being foreclosed and is thus said from 'no part' or 'nowhere' as Messiah-in-Person. There are many aspects to the signifying and the signified relation, taking one particular scission among others, but each and every adumbration arises from an identity that is, importantly, *not* a performative, as if one could interpret a confession of faith in linguistic terms and claim that the Man (of) faith was merely a believing animal; on the contrary, faith is an already-performed, without any constituent act, ritual or sacramental performance. While there certainly has been such an act, there is no single constitutive and 'originary' one. The identity of a faithful confession rests much less upon a banal and indeterminate ontological unity, which, from this perspective and according to this measure, could give rise to a deconstruction, than upon a faith that is radically subtracted from language and gives rise, instead, to confessional axiom-symbols. Faith subtracts itself from the synthesis of the doublet and, in the end, from the Word, as well as from the identity of the sign and sense, that explains the 'play of language'. If there is an indivisible identity that amounts to a being in-Identity, then this would be the identity of faith or the faithful Man, without any predicates or object(s). The symbols of faith are like axioms, not mathematical but real, that arise from decisions that do not relate to any object but rather 'in-bring' the religious insofar as non-religious.

Faith transforms the works of the world

When recognized as faith-world or belief without fidelity, the old faith is an artefact set in conjunction with three determinations: (1) a mythological and religious foundation, marked by divine transcendence; (2) the event of Christ that determines this foundation, regardless of any particular historicity, and so prolongs the division between the earthly or terrestrial history, which concerns the structures and rituals of the Church, and salvation history; and (3) finally, a conceptual and scriptural (or theological) synthesis. Faith is attributed to man under this triple constraint and marks a contingent predicate for an anthropologico-rational subject that takes the sole form of a violent attribution undertaken by the Church and theology in the name of faith that cannot really relate in any way to Man. An administered faith sanctions according to an 'indifference with regard to religious matters'. Faith is no longer a category of the religious, encircled, if not reached, by the power of the concept, which remains in all rigour ineffable or absurd. Such attributions and predicates (the works, writings, procedures) divide and tear Man apart; they distribute Man to all four corners of transcendence. By dividing Man in this way, they redouble and reflect the world – the social returns under the form of the ecclesial and the biological under the form of the body of the Church.

Dogmas are only opinions founded upon the totality or the form of the world, through mythologies of the letter, language, and representation that faith must liberate. Within a faith that has been converted or transformed into a religion, the risen Christ is understood in terms of an anticipated object. From this understanding follows an eventual appropriation of the risen Christ by a dialectic. When faith refuses such a conversion into religion, however, and, instead, uni–verses, then this gives rise to the non-religious. The non-religious accompanies, like an effect, the Man (of) faith, who grants this much like a grace that he has not received. The subject, moreover, can receive the call of the religious as a solicitation or an occasional cause, inviting him or her to the living memory and actions of Christ. The Resurrection does not re-engage a process of eternal return or repetition but rather a process of transformation of the old faith, that is, the belief in fables and mythologies that have been manipulated for the benefit of the Church.

If I were to confess 'my' faith on the basis of the foregoing, then this would be only insofar as a religious subject. This is, however, precisely what intimates me through the force of speech or via a speaking in-the-last-instance, not through any concept, prayer, or edifying story but rather via a certain kind of decision that is ordered according to axioms. It is not done on the basis of theological theses but rather axioms that can make use of prayer, concepts, edifying stories, and dogmas that organize the old faith. If faith is the new terrain yet makes no change at all, then the writing, speech, and 'scriptures' that comprise faith must assume a new form. They remain *aspects* of a thesis or decision but are, importantly, no longer founded upon the perspective or hypothesis of the transcendence of divine salvation – a second creation that is still lacking even a first – and a religious history of a promise. They rest, instead, upon the immanent being-given of faith, necessary, but insufficient, in order to create a dogma, and so a being-revealed of Man insofar as separated from the World and religion. This is not an opinion raised to the state of a truth that is imposed by the structures of the Church. If the Man (of) faith is true, as a necessary but insufficient condition, then Man could transform existing dogmas into truths insofar as works of faith. The Gospel of the Man (of) faith only makes use of biblical scripture as a simple given (or *datum*) that hides, like a symptom, a possible core for knowing and truth that only axiomatic symbols can extract and exhibit. Axioms ordered according to faith form a theoretical liturgy and practice that is adapted to the intrinsic finitude of Man rather than God – only through grace can Man, in virtue of faith, give to the world and to religions.

Two affirmations must be held together in a unilateral manner: *faith is without object but nevertheless brings about the non-religious on the occasion of religion.* We cannot be content with simply reversing the domination of religion over faith in order to affirm the intimate or interior character of a pietist faith. On the contrary, this concerns faith as the radical Inverse, which does not itself have a place – an inversion that precipitates religion outside of itself in the simple non-religious. Far from withdrawing or abstracting itself from the world, faith abstracts itself in such a radical manner that it thus transforms religion and emancipates the human subject. In the truth that is proper to faith, beyond theological knowledge, and the work most proper to it, beyond the works of the 'death of religion', lies the salvation of the subject in-world by the Man (of) faith. Salvation is only a human emancipation with respect to the transcendence of God, who is not a watchmaker or architect, like the old mechanisms of belief, but the 'key stone' of Church structures or their pretension to auto-function. The absence at the heart of the tomb empties the sufficiency of religions; it is the action proper to the non-act of Christ and the determining force of the axiomatic decision, inverting prayer or edification into decision.

Faith testifies to a forced speech

Who speaks in confession? To speak and confess have almost nothing in common other than the common unity of language. Confession does not consist in speaking like a Christian on the basis of language in general. This is precisely what philosophy does, posing Man as the rational animal or logos, and, likewise, what Christianity believes when speaking about 'professions' of faith – a formula that indicates only too well the alienating mixture of Man with the world, perpetuating the original religious sin against Man. Confession indicates a radical difference in the structure that underpins the use of language. Faith does not speak directly, under pain of alienating itself, without hope of any return, in the language-world, or even at the risk of confusing Man with the speaking subject. Faith does not manipulate symbols, the subject, and its two aspects, like an ensemble of relations between language and the world; rather, faith employs a faithful subject that assumes Man-in-Person or in-faith. The subject confesses their faith through the transformation of the religious, without being itself confessed. The very modern confusion between confessing faith or speaking according to faith and making a confession about oneself must be refused along with the confusion between the work of faith *for* the world and work of the subject-world *in* the world. Even faith does not 'confess' itself: the kind of identity and immanence that belongs to faith does not make this possible – it is not at all subjective. Doubtless, the subject makes use of the means furnished by religions and theologies but does so only when forced in-the-last-instance by faith. We suggest that the subject is forced twice, if not within a double language, then at least a double constraint. This is true, certainly, but the forces are not the same. The first is the force of language and the linguistic, which is at once immanent and transcendent. But this becomes merely occasional. The other is an intimation or ultimation made by Christ to and within the subject, and eventually assumed by it. This intimation arises from a faith more intimate to me than myself (*interior intimo me*) – Man as an immanence that is more radical than any interiority in the world (*Homo interior intimo meo*). The forced intimacy of faith for the subject, ceaselessly coming once each time, means this is an ultimation, that is, a constitutive ultimatum of human intimacy and constitutive of the subject. Faith is the Real – the non-explicable and non-definable that must be understood solely as the intimate ultimatum that forces instituted language and religion, 'exceeding' them only by 'transforming' them into a theo-fiction.

The symbol of faith is without-relation, joining faithful speech to the void and the religious occasion that accompanies it. In the old use of the symbol, there is an indivisible identity, a first division, and then a hazardous and fortunate reunion of two parts, separated and thrown into the vast world. If this duality is accentuated in order to emphasize once again and in a definitive manner its impossible unity, resting this upon an occasional and chance instance in terms of the miracle-in-person – the effect of faith upon mountains – then the sense and meaning of the symbol changes and loses any worldly and religious exteriority. Such an axiom, drawing together two incommensurable yet identical parts in-the-last-fidelity (faith and the religion-world), marks the symbol (of) faith, that is, the immanent miracle of the encounter between fidelity and the world, the uni-que cry ('Jesus!'), that is the symbolic void or the axiom and theorem of the work striking at the heart of the world. At the foundation of prayer, which expresses faith and insists in the axiom, lies, in the most rigorous sense, the *real* possibility of the miracle. Man (of) faith unifies what religions separate.

2

The Gospels: Models for non-Christianity

A Gnostic Christ and the insurrection of faith

Why invoke Christianity? What is its function in this generic context? A religious conjuncture is necessary in order to confess 'its' faith and transform a worldly, religious substance into an immanent symbol. Christianity is the dominant conjuncture for the subject who speaks here and confesses their faith, not only as Man-in-Person, certainly – Man not being a religious animal – but also as a subject within the limits of the human. This is evidently a contingent conjuncture that affords only an occasion for 'dis-alienation' from a dominant mode of subjection. Moreover, since Christianity is a religion set within a special historical and theoretical position, surpassing other religions in their sole mode of transcendence – that is, natural or Judaic – from *within*, making divine and anonymous religious foundations appear as counterfeit mythological and pagan 'backdrops', this prepares the way for a human theology. 'Whoever has seen me has seen the Father' (John 14:9). This almost suffices or at least suffices for 'me' in order to send the terrible God of monotheism back into the obscure ethnomythological ground, that is, back towards a bad faith, understood as belief. This is not, however, a surpassing, overcoming, or *Aufhebung* in an Hegelian manner; it is not a question here of converting (or sublating) religion into Absolute Spirit or even into Man but rather converting Man into what *uni–verts* religion and de-sacralizes faith. Far from being the accomplishment of religion, in the sense of its end or final convocation, the notion of a human theology brings religion to an ultimatum: Man as the first of last things or the last of first things – that is, according to the past or the future. Hegel speaks of the end of art for the benefit of aesthetics, must one speak today about Christianity being the end of religion and the triumph of a new theology – that is, the philosophy of the Absolute Spirit? On the contrary, we announce, instead, the Kingdom of Man and the end of religious and theological times. This theme, though, haunts a number of humanist theologies emerging within German thought (e.g. Feuerbach) like a symptom. For all these reasons, Christianity is a symptom to be welcomed, gathered together, and harvested. In posing the equation *Man = Man (of) faith* and seeking the root of faith not in God but in Christ, we utilize Christianity in order to prepare the way for the most significant revolution or overturning initiated, in particular, by this claim: *Christ Himself will no longer be the root of faith, but its interpretative model.*

We are, for the moment, in an ambiguous conjuncture. By granting a certain primacy to the decision of faith over and above unitary monotheism(s), Christianity brings the divine to the point of being withdrawn before Man. This Christian retreat is not the death of God, but His *survival*. God has suffered the most modern, even too-modern, fate: He is a Survivor reduced to silence. This retreat, if well understood, must not give rise, once again, to the modern and overly hasty ideology of the 'death of God' – well known to philosophers; rather, the Christian God is pushed as far as entering the pallid and cadaverous state of a survivor in the company of the hallucinatory subject of Absolute

Subjectivity and humanist and humanist conceptions of man, which is also on the way back towards an immemorial past. Deciphered thus on the basis of a new faith and in terms that determine or clone the religious subject, starting from a positive religion, Christianity represents the first lineaments of an incomplete transplantation of the faith-world on to a new terrain of non-Christianity.

Indeed, it is possible to speak of this in terms of a task that transplants belief into the immanence of faith. Yet, once Man has lost all his attributes, and his faith no longer has the same 'quality', but rather deprives him of each and every quality, upon what terrain does Man stand? What is the destination or the place that tearing the decision of faith away from the transcendent gods of paganism as well as the monotheistic Unique God or Great God, Most-High or Most-Great, makes possible? Such questions offer one more reason to look within the tortured and fractured surroundings of Christianity and Judaism: Gnosticism. Gnosis represents the most innovative and heretical aspect to Christianity, that is, the vision of man as an autonomous being, more real than the world, and separated, in essence, from it. Gnosticism requires a 'dis-alienation' of man from the world.

Touching upon the archaic foundations of religion, it is not possible to overestimate the importance of the gnostic cut or disconnection from such foundations, which can make Gnosticism appear like a mythological delirium, while, in fact, it only causes religion to appear so. Generally rejected, hated, or mocked in established Christianity over the course of centuries, the 'gnostic cut' can now be resumed here as the threshold for an heretical un-blocking of religions. This threshold arises in the midst of a rupture between the jealous and, above all, 'wicked' God of the Old Testament, author of a botched creation, on one side, without doubt celebrated by philosophers and theologians in their respective theodicies, and Christ as the figure of a potentially good God, on the other, who will grant to Man an art or practice of faith. We are close to admitting that a non-philosophical confession of faith must accord the same degree of importance to the permanent crucifixion of the gnostics as one does to the crucifixion of Christ and the continual persecution of the Jews, even though their respective fates, as victims, differ markedly. Each offers a paradigmatic crime against Man.

The gnostic cut into religion is, in any case, an initiation into a new intelligence, showing at once the value of generic faith and its capacity to defrock the religious. If this is, indeed, a certain type of monotheism, then there is nothing in common between the most fully developed or least regressive Christianity, on one side, and Judaism, on the other; there has, however, been an incubation period – a phase of Judaeo-Christian continuum – that progressively breaks down into pieces yet nevertheless returns, under different symptoms, into society and philosophy. This rupture that so many Christians would secretly like to see fulfilled is far from being accomplished. The accomplishment or realization of this rupture no longer takes the form of a distended continuity or Judea-Christian allergy but an *inversion of Judaism by Christ, understood in terms of gnosticism*. The insurrection of faith, foreclosed or forbidden in advance to every belief, now sets the Glorious 'Resurrection' of Christ in opposition to the vampire-like 'cadaverization' of the surviving Jewish God. Is it now incumbent upon us – we-the-faithful of no religion, the without-religion – to renounce the memory of this God or to resuscitate Him? Since God has not even risen, we introduce, by every possible means, a positive religion to the Man (of) faith along with the subject of non-religion.

The words of Jesus on life

Before commenting on St Paul, it is necessary to elucidate the theoretical status of the sayings of Jesus, which have often been treated with a certain 'popular' or 'orientalizing' condescension. Setting to one side all prior arguments concerning the 'mediating' role of Jesus and His universion or dualysis as medium-without-mediation, His message itself, before any Pauline reprise, assumes the function of nomination or consecration, developed in a few very simple formulae, which could very well be taken for axioms and must, indeed, be maintained as such – for example 'whoever has seen me, has seen the Father' (John, 14: 9) or even the quasi-axioms of the 'beatitudes' given in the Sermon on the Mount. Such formulae on life and the living, the importance of which Michel Henry identified and discerned, must be determined and set against all evidence, admitted and maintained against all the powers and hierarchies currently in place. From this point of view, the nomination of the 'Happy' and the 'Simple' to whom life has been promised or announced contests the Pauline nomination with respect to the 'Resurrection'. There is, doubtless, a difference between Jesus or His promise of life, on one side, and the Resurrected or Risen, on the other, in terms of the efficacy of this promise. But, on the one hand, the promise of Jesus cannot be in itself a simple 'fable' at the level of empirical fact – it is kerygmatic – and, on the other, St Paul can only confirm another belief, which, if there had not been a prior promise made by Jesus, would be, in fact, a purely voluntarist nomination. Could there be an event without a minimal promise, that is, without its prior announcement? This would be a pure act, not only without support in a given situation but also lacking any content. The nomination is nothing – a breath, an absolutely void intention, decidedly too void, or even an intention sufficient in itself and for itself – without a non-empirical condition amounting to an *a priori* of the promise. The promises and proclamations of Jesus form an *a priori* under which are set the conditions for human life in the world. Put another way, the Pauline affirmation of the Resurrection finds itself so deprived of an *a priori* foundation that it could only emanate from the will of a philosopher or theologian *ex machina*, seizing the real event of Jesus in terms of Christ and then denying this event as mere 'fable' in order better to assure mastery over it. The Pauline affirmation intends to define (philosophically and theologically) the meaning of this event, whereas Jesus already constitutes by Himself its meaning in terms of a promise that is proximate to the Resurrection. The supposition that the Word of Jesus, that is, what He says or means, may be an illuminated fable changes nothing with respect to the revolutionary force of such statements. Just like St Paul's statements concerning the Resurrection, those made by Jesus regarding life and the living put to work a fidelity and an insistence; and, in doing so, they make the Resurrection much better understood than the mere affirmation of its name 'Resurrection'.

The sayings of Jesus: Theorems or axioms?

What is the theoretical status of these formulae on the living and the promise of life? The most fundamental words on humanity are at the same time the most brief, teetering at the limit of tautology, without any socio-historic foundation to assure or legitimate them. The very succinct character of what Jesus says, if variations are taken to be simply anecdotal and historical, reveals a general and fundamental brevity, which stands in contrast to the eloquent rhetoric of St Paul.

What remains for us to accomplish now is a dualysis of Jesus' sayings. At the moment, the force of Jesus' sayings is felt without any clarity regarding their theoretical status. An elucidation of their theoretical status is necessary in order to tear them from their 'calming' or 'soothing' character as well as from their possible interpretation along lines we nevertheless come to defend, albeit provisionally in anticipation of a coming dualysis. This is all the more necessary in order better to assure the seriousness of the 'real' – a provisional defence, in terms of nomination, which must be founded, at the most minimal level, on the promise. Besides, we said 'a proximate promise' or 'near promise' and spoke of their quasi-axiomatic character. This is the nub of these problems and precisely what needs to be elucidated, at least in their most essential characteristics.

In reality, the Church has always received the words of Jesus as a kind of axiom – that is, made actual or effective by faith or the teaching of the Church, belief and dogma. The interpretation of the Words on Life (Jesus) given by a philosopher like Henry suspends any sense of transcendence supposed in them, lifting them out from dogmas and belief, and setting them within the immanence of Life, which generates its own intelligence, without founding itself externally in the worldly support of the Church. But Henry does not free them completely from their surreptitious foundation in transcendence. His interpretation only manages to pose a radical immanence in a restricted form by means of an external gesture or operation – that is, *a philosophical one* – upon another philosophy that is shorn off from its real structure. This operation allows him to pose an immanence, doubtless, but only a transcendental one. It is not, therefore, surprising that Henry's Christianity resolves itself into a Christo-centrism, a centre from which Life can recognize divine transcendence precisely as a transcendence experienced in immanence. In a sense, such an interpretation is 'faithful' to the words of the historical Christ: 'whoever has seen me, has seen the Father.' But those of us who do not share this fidelity, that is, who are not Christian, cannot reconstruct a classical Christo-centrism starting from Christ; it is as though immanence must remain transcendental and never reach as far as Man-in-Person, who, for us, bearing faith, sub-tends immanence, whereas, for our philosopher, the worldly man remains the subject of faith, called 'Christian'. From our perspective, there is no longer any centre or periphery, no more God than Christ; there is Real-Man, appointed subject-Christ in order to struggle against the world and the transcendence that enslaves him. Christianity is, at best, Christo-centrism. However, we seek a Christo-fiction, which completes the 'Henrian' uprooting of the subject-Christ out from the substance of transcendence and, instead, roots him in Man-without-Substance.

What does the persistence of transcendence signify, if not an interpretation of the words of Christ in terms of theorems, explaining faith, legislating upon it – that is, upon the Real – and, subsequently, developing into a series of dogmas, more constrictive and deadly than any other? Such theorems are, one could doubtless say, believed and founded upon faith. But this remains a mixed or concocted faith, transcendent of Christian philosophy. A belief considers, in its own way, axioms to be quasi-theorems, possessing an intuitive content and empirical validity that orders or regulates human life from the Heavens. In reality, the sayings of Jesus are really only axioms that decide Christ. Yet in order to see them according to this status, the vicious circle, where a Christian interpretation of such statements founds Christianity – that is, faith interpreting faith or auto-justifying itself – must be renounced. What matters here is a progress towards a uni–version, that is, an operation tracing or establishing the sayings of Jesus as simple axioms and formulae, possessing an *a priori* concrete content understood to be 'material', but human or immanent. They are thus able to engender the Word called, in this case, Christo-fiction, which undoes the philosophical presuppositions of Christo-centrism or Christology, underpinning multiple doctrinal variants. Parallel to this effort, but by other means, the empirico-transcendental Christian dogmatic, which suffuses and innervates all Christologies with their own philosophical *animus*, will be used as a simple model for Christ-fiction. Withdrawing Christianity from the false axioms that it previously granted the status of theorems, we establish *for the first time, in a non-historical manner*, the purely axiomatic character of these sayings that determine in-the-last-instance only a non-Christian Word – an invention of human or delivered life. This amounts to no less than the construction of a veritable non-Christianity, theoretically more rigorous and more universal, less empirical, that is, less worldly, and so delivered from servitude to the Church.

More profoundly dogmatic (in the broader sense and in order to simplify), the foundation of Christianity poses a reversibility between the Church and subjects, between Christians and faithful subjects, between dogma and faith – they are, in each pair, the 'same'. Without doubt, this formulation is a gross simplification, forgetting the artful nuances and techniques of distinctions developed by the Church and its theologians. But we consider precisely such seemingly benign growths and excrescences to be part of a spontaneous cancer, so-to-speak, of Christian theology – a cancer upon the Mystical Body, once and each time for the faithful; it is an artifice that precipitates a devastating indifference or dis-engagement, namely, religions that engage in such 'scholastic' activities. Moreover, the simplification of the theoretical structure of dogma is not without use when we treat them as simply material or symptoms for a dualysis, which will discern and outline the lineaments of a wholly different structure, namely 'non-Christian', simpler still than dogma. For good reason, therefore, yet often difficult to discern, Christian dogma is 'parmenidian' or philosophical; it poses this reversibility, with numerous, yet useless, differences, between faith and the Christian subject, between fidelity and the ecclesial community. No one can be called 'Christian' if he or she does not recognize the Church (or at least *a* Church), that is, if he or she does not belong to one. Such co-belonging is immediately, as ever, hierarchical and political. The Church grants subjects their Christian status, sense, and predicate; God, then Christ, delivers to the Church its ultimate credentials.

Philosophy, Christian dogma, and, perhaps, the modern state, in the broadest sense, possess the same structure, namely the form of transcendental reciprocal equation.

Why does Christ, in this whole affair, remain worldly? Did Christ not come precisely in order to the change the ancient, old givens, even going as far as making God – the ancient, jealous God – struggle to recognize Himself in Christianity? What does the 'death of God' mean, simply as a phenomenon, beyond established commentary or any historico-sociological considerations, and apart from a cause for rejoicing amongst atheists? Christ is evidently the 'pivot' or the 'key point' for Christianity, binding human subjects to religious transcendence. From this follows, however, a new symptom, apparent in the religious sphere, where nothing really functions any more within this structure. Christ is the Great Disruptor of religions, setting the stakes for this struggle, no longer a war of religions but a fight of Man against all religions. His sayings, historically, in the end, so impoverished, need to be interpreted in accordance with His person, that is, in terms of His immanence as the last Son of Man, rather than viciously and circularly constituted via Christian auto-justification. These sayings are, then, the possibility and chance to 'decapitate' the subjects of transcendence, that is, liberate messiahs from the heavy and weighty presence of the Father. Deciding in favour of radical immanence and against the uselessness of the transcendence of the Father, the *a priori* transcendental equation of the Church is broken, at least what remains of this with St Paul or finds itself amplified therein – that is, the equation that poses the Father and the Son, faith and belief as *the same, but hierarchically or unequally so*. This equation amounts to a theological theorem, but a rectified one, having now been reduced to axioms that engender it, saying precisely this: the Father and the Son are identical in-the-last-paternity, that is, in-the-last-humanity. Christ is the messiah who brings, without creating, this impasse; He is the subject charged with the mission to block or set in impasse Christian theology.

It should now be clear that this operation does not simply transform and extend the Christian Word to a 'non-Euclidian' theoretical universality; it is only preparatory for what surpasses or sets in impasse any and every operation. This operation also allows us to grasp Man-in-Person in terms of an infinite and non-divine immanence and the subject in terms of a Son of Man-in-Person or a universal messiah, who arrives for the first time, that is, once each time. In fact, our Word is already actual here, that is, determined in-the-last-humanity, and forced to this universality of subject-messiahs that *we* are already.

Life, living, surviving, and glorious experience

What is the relation between the axiomatic style and the Gospels? The necessity of the axiom is motivated, in part, by the canonic Gospels, without speaking here of the apocryphal, gnostic ones. But such axioms are not founded upon them. Far from being the foundation that would justify this form, which, as an aside, cannot find any justification in their empirico-historic character, they are, instead, the model for the quasi-axiomatic posture of faith. Our relation to the 'founding' or 'inspirational' texts must be *inverted*, not reversed. They can be read in at least two ways, through which their identity, understood as the duality of two messages, is postulated and determined in history either in terms of 'philosophies of life' or in terms of mystics, understood to imitate Christ's suffering. On the one hand, they can be understood as calls or appeals to the living, that is, a popular and positive message of a new life, oscillating between exhortation and edification; they are 'simple' and 'happy' discourses (from which Henry has drawn the phenomenological consequences, albeit as the announcement of an immanent Life, carrying the auto-revelatory power of Life outside the world). On the other hand, they can be read with respect to the necessity of death, that is, as the well-known sequence of the passion announced at Cana, then through the crucifixion, the placing in the tomb, and the discovery of the empty tomb (from which St Paul has drawn the consequences, albeit in terms of a Life as the object of Resurrection, passing through the essential moment of death solely in order to overcome it). These two messages differ in their sense and have given rise to diverse interpretations, opposed in their presuppositions, namely Revelation or Resurrection. From the perspective of radical Man, namely our non-phenomenological view, they signify together (but without synthesis or dialectical 'overcoming' [*Aufhebung*]) that the new 'Life' that is Christ is not of this world; it is empty of the world and interrupts or breaks the regime of religions and their mythology. But then it is also empty of 'life'. The very concept of 'Life' is no longer sufficient and no longer has any place here. The concept of Life is only a philosophical mask beneath which something else announces itself. From this point of view, the real content of Life is *Lived-without-life*, the Non-living-lived, or, even further still, the non-surviving. Even under the elaborated and phenomenological form of Life and Living (Henry), such a message will only be a *model* for a radically immanent Life, that is, an historico-philosophical interpretation of the Glorious Lived, forming the (philosophical) sense and meaning that adds itself to the generic non-religious structure.

One could, of course, reconcile, in general, much like Hegel, the message of death and the message of life in the *Aufhebung* of the Resurrection and ascension to Heaven. It is, of course, possible to take hold of a dialectical form there, with all its diverse moments:

the negation of immediate life by law, death as the negation of negation, and, in the end, the identity of the death of death in the Resurrection as a 'superior' Life. Rather than imagine a dialectical process, beginning necessarily with the Law, understood as the death of immediate life, we see, instead, in this logico-historical structure, the most universal and anti-dialectical generic axiom, wherein the two sources or symbols – that is, life and death – stand only as two moments, not three. Death is thus only unilateral and turned against the mixture or concoction of life-death (i.e. the world), accomplished through the philosophical concept of 'life'; it is the Glorious Living, which does not alienate itself in the world but rather uses death only against the influence of the world. Death does not affect the Glorious Living, only the mixture of life with death. This marks a return to the Gospels in their role as model, interpreting here a generic 'formal' posture. In order to 'formalize' this duality in a human mode, it must be posed *as an indivisible duality but in a single discourse or message* – namely, life – but life understood as dying to the world or, put another way, as Glorious Living. What we call fidelity is identical to immanent or faithful 'life', not phenomenological life. It is the Lived-without-life that makes the Man (of) faith. With regard to death and the empty tomb, it is the living tomb or the tomb empty of death itself! Both are needed for this New Life or even New Lived and its immanence. Death cannot be first; it cannot enjoy any primacy – that is, form the essence of life, since doing so would return life to the philosophical process of survival (e.g. dialectical overcoming). Death can be the guardian of life; it can be included in 'life' as the way new life manifests itself for the world. Life and death do not form a synthesis, any more than belief and faith; death is not negation, even double negation (i.e. the negation of negation), understood as the condition of life. Rather, death symbolizes the being-separated and non-worldly status of life. *Dying to the world is also immanent and does not dialectically contradict life. It does not have its place in the tomb; rather, this New Life or a priori must die in the eyes of the world, but its death must be 'dead'*. No longer a double death – death of death – via an objective dialectical appearance, death is, from the outset and in essence, Lived Gloriously in-the-last-instance. Life and death form a unilateral duality. Each must be included, even death, as Lived, which retains an aspect of death, but a dualyzed one, turned against itself. Death separates the Lived, which is the essence of death, and distinguishes it from world-death, that is, from survival. It is here that Christ is radically distinguished as the Glorious Risen, without Resurrection, wholly separated from survival, which is a philosophico-Judaic interpretation of Man.

This simple death, as opposed to a complex 'double death', belongs now to Man-in-Man and ought not to be confused with an event recounted in an anecdotal manner, like the surprise of Mary and Martha before the empty tomb. Simple death is the condition for the manifestation of the non-religious transcendental ideality in which Christ transformed His faith, namely the worldly and legislative religion of His ancestors. The Resurrection among the dead would have no need to found a new religion but rather institute the non-religion that *there is*.... The Logos loses any claim to incarnate the Real, which now flees into and finds refuge in faith; it is reduced to the body of Christ, that is, set in memory or the empty tomb. We refuse to sublate or overcome, in a dialectical manner, the body of Christ, whose 'real absence' is precisely what prevents any such overcoming. The Gospels prepare the way for a rebellion against religion and no longer gather together the conditions needed for a positive (or even negative) theology. They 'model' or interpret a non-theology, which is a way of thinking that renders justice to faith as determining cause, thereby inverting religion. This is the stake from a generic or non-theological point of view: not to reverse religions but rather to invert them in the name of Man (of) faith. The kerygma of Christ has been twisted, turned, and recuperated for the profit of the most inhuman transcendence. Christ is the death and Resurrection of all metaphysics and phenomenology of Life, the Living, and, above all, the Surviving – there is a new 'life' for them here, too. It is too simplistic to believe that Christ marks a simple and straightforward refusal of philosophy or even its condemnation; rather, Christ is foreclosed to philosophy in order better to save it from itself.

Christ according to St Paul: The Pauline reversal

These two roots of Christianity, which, as we have argued, form only one, in an unequal equality or unilateral way, form an authentic structure or real content for what has been distorted and deranged in the form of Christianity. Christ-the-Gnostic has been interpreted prematurely, too hastily, alongside another, namely the 'Christian' Christ. The two evangelical roots, in their unilateral duality, have been divided, each mutually doubling the other, and at the same time accompany the emergence of a third destiny, founding the possibility for a philosophical and theological system. This other source is St Paul and his deathly inspiration. While this inspiration is doubtless set forth in the name of the 'Risen', it nevertheless reduces this to an operation and, in doing so, leads it back from 'glorious' death to world-death and the dialectic. Such an inspiration underscores either the Resurrection of life or the mortal conditions that precede the Resurrection. In both cases, the duality is conserved. We see no reason to avoid or condemn the interpretations put forward by Hegel and Nietzsche and isolate the single order-word 'Resurrection', thus highlighted and supposed to be without common measure with death or sacrifice (Badiou).

Only a decision in favour of caesura and rupture, inspired by an ultra-voluntarist theory of a supernumerary nomination of the event called 'Resurrection', however, could impose a twist and torsion upon the texts of St Paul, making them the 'foundation for a universalism' that is especially abstract with regard to any and every historical situation, and so only justifiable on the basis that the event itself or its content is declared, through this nomination, a 'fable' (Badiou). The words of life spoken by Christ would thus be considered a fable, while the words of St Paul would not be so. Moreover, such an interpretation, which, as an aside, would hold good, were it not abusively attributed to St Paul, insists, rightly, upon the duality of life and death, that is, upon a certain hesitation of the Apostle, which would lead directly to a dialectical interpretation, rather than a 'material' one. The way of death would hold good only for the immanent material conditions for the situation – that is, the 'site' of the event called 'Resurrection'. What is interesting about this interpretation revolves around the way in which it pulls apart the supposed dialectic of St Paul (the philosopher-idealist) via materialism. But in this spirit of materialism – but spiritual this time – another possible critique of Pauline Christianity still stands, one which would no longer privilege the Resurrection as an operation seized by religions but rather the Risen Himself, thereby affirming that He is the presupposition of the Resurrection. Such a critique would seek the immanent conditions by way of life this time, not death – that is, the radical Lived, which can 'support' or determine in-the-last-instance the Resurrection of the body. Far from bodies being simply 'earthen vessels' destined to collect and gather the Resurrection, only then to allow this to escape from or overflow all parts, they would insofar as set within a radical immanence, already glorious and radiant, bring the Resurrection, that is, the salvation of the world. Within this framework, where the Risen assumes primacy, death takes on an altogether different sense, namely as an *a priori* condition for who- or whatever grants salvation, that is, 'death' as *a priori* material for salvation, rather than a simple material condition for a nomination (Badiou). True immanence is lived and radical, one could even say 'spiritual' if one preferred; it is not material, but nevertheless capable of being deployed as such. The Resurrection is an operation or a nomination by which religions and remnants of this in philosophy capture Humans and turn them into survivors. But the Risen, on the contrary, radiates *a priori* salvation, that is, 'being-living'.

St Paul is the Apostle who sets the Resurrection above the Risen, even above the Lived, placing the operation above the Real and, in doing so, revives belief at the expense of faith. In the role of the Great Recuperator, the apostle objectively presupposes a vast synthesis of the Judaic and Greek, oscillating between the two. A new religion, called 'Christianity', is thus born from the dialectical spirit, hesitating between life and death, in a struggle with itself and others. The apostle prefers the 'message of death' and rests upon this basis – that is, the primacy of death – the supposed New Life of the Resurrection, constituting a religious normalization of the Christian message. The entire difference between theology and non-theology, between belief and faith, can be found here in this confusion between the Resurrection as an event – either articulated via a dialectic or affirmed in an abstract manner – and the Risen-without-Resurrection. This is, in short, the difference between life and the Lived-without-life. Christ is born-without-birth; He is the Risen-in-Person, who does not depend upon an operation of Resurrection, enacted by God as a second creation – the first being evidently insufficient, thereby necessitating an idealized doubling or reduplication. St Paul thus founds Christianity – a new religion – upon the Resurrection of someone dead and 'among the dead' by misunderstanding the primacy of the Lived and life over and above death. The 'Pauline turn' determines a particular historico-worldly possibility for Christian kerygma, binding the latter closely to the former. Rather than understand and interpret the historic Gospels as models or 'interpretations' for this kerygma of faith, St Paul does so *empirically and in a predominantly Judaic manner. They are understood solely in terms of their given status, that is, as empirically auto-justifying, and, consequently, an idealizing and Greco-philosophical conclusion is drawn concerning faith in Christ, as risen among the dead. The apostle idealizes Jesus and transforms Him into a model, in the philosophical or Platonic sense (model-copy), rather than an interpretative model for a formal structure. Such an idealizing interpretation gives rise to a dialectical or a materialist hiatus (death).* This is a classic and habitual vicious turn of thought that confines itself solely to the authority of history or texts rather than establish any structure and authority on its human roots, which impose the primacy of faith upon the works of the world.

Christian theology and philosophies of religion – in short, any transcendent universalism, whether idealist or materialist – indeed, whatever is not rooted in the Glorious Body but, instead, in conceptual entities, arise from St Paul and the barely perceptible twists and torsions made by him with respect to the initial kerygma of Jesus. This marks a turn toward an idealizing Christianity, and, therefore, in another manner, a 'deathly' turn of thought. With Hegel and, more recently, even Henry, in some partial sense at least, theology treats the Gospels, in particular, the story of the empty tomb, in a manner that is far too historical and positive, and, consequently, almost as a corollary, too metaphorical, for philosophical discourse, which decides faith insofar as a relation to the world of religion. If death and the void are understood as effects of the Glorious Body, that is, effects of an *a priori*, then the latter can be seen to undermine the dialectical and conceptual for the benefit of a single and unique Survival-without-surviving, which contains the 'death of religion' and, perhaps, even its glorious life. If the event called 'Christ' is understood in 'formal', rather than ideal, terms, that is, understood solely with respect to its *real* nature, then religion can be seen only to conserve the ideality of the non-religious or the transcendental memory of Christ. The void of Christ, that is, the scene at the empty tomb, determines the religious, more so even than a simple retreat or ascension to Heaven. But it does so only on condition that the events of the Lived are not confused with an overcoming or a discursive operation. Christ introduces faith as a real object of religion, replacing those of the most ancient beliefs – a faith that the latter distort and mask. He permits the rejection of the entire power of the concept and philosophical reflection in the name of the Man (of) faith. The ascent to Heaven and the Resurrection are a new way or mode for the *there is* of the religious – not a new religion, rather a new non-religion.

The Torah, rather than being simply the religious ground from which Christianity arose, is the religious foundation that it needed to transform. But Pauline Christianity nevertheless installs itself within this transcendent religious milieu under the form of a struggle against the Jews and the Law, that is, in an opposition to the Torah rather than in the posture of a transformation. It paves the way for a reconstitution of religion, pressing upon the world the essential forms of religious domination. The Pauline emancipation of men is incomplete, even botched, according to the Gnostics, for the same schematic reason: an excess of transcendence. The major divisions and distinctions – between polytheism and monotheism, between Judaism and Christianity, between Jesus and St Paul – are, in the end, hardly novel until their syntax is unilaterally oriented and specified. It is, for example, scarcely of any significance that St Paul's retelling of Tacitus' formula regarding the Jews, namely, that they would carry 'the hatred of human kind', gives rise to an historical hypothesis for or against an interpolation; it is merely a symptom of the author. But on the condition of making human kind the pivot for a new confession that orders Man, rather than the inverse, Man ceases to be a subject to which attributes of this type might be given; it is Man, indeed, without belonging to this class or receiving such an attribution, who determines them. Man is accompanied by the kind of universal that is foreclosed to such predication and attribution, and thereby foreclosed to itself as well, unable to determine but nevertheless able to grant its own identity. Understood in this way, the thematic of the 'hatred of humankind' could be generalized to every religion and philosophy, whose anthropology certainly cannot be extricated from its responsibility. But this would only narrow philosophical and generic operations.

St Paul according to Jesus: The Pauline inversion

Let us take the inverse route, moving this time from St Paul to Christ. The question regarding the origins of Christianity has given rise to interminable discussion: Jesus or St Paul? The 'alternative' – that is, the disjunction either/or – must be refused here. It testifies only to an incomprehension, typically historical and philosophical, before the great inventions and, furthermore, before an anticipated theologico-worldly contraction or diminution. There are, in fact, two distinct sources of Christianity, understood as an historical religion. Each fulfils different and specific functions. One of them is the message of the new life announced by Jesus. This is given in the midst of Judaism and strikes at the heart of an ancient problem, which, at the time, must remain essentially misunderstood. It is an innovative and ambiguous moment, like an incomprehensible discovery in the religious field, wherein this novel announcement is made, yet remains theoretically inassimilable in the context of reception, meaning it can only take the twists and turns of a sect. It cannot be emphasized enough just how much the problem of scientific, philosophical, and theological reception is so often too quick and lacks sufficient awareness of their respective phenomena. This hastiness reduces discoveries and inventions to the norms of their reception and the resultant antinomies. The second factor, articulated with the first around the axis of the Resurrection, concerns the universalizing effect of St Paul's message, which, without the prior message of new life, given by Jesus, would be only an empty speech, resonating within the hollows of a bell. The alternative Jesus or St Paul is, then, absurd in every way. Every invention develops or unfolds in two distinct phases: the first is, of course, discovery; the second is the universalization of this discovery and its structures in the theoretical field of reception.

But universalization can operate in two ways: reversal and inversion. The first is generalization, idealization, and the *reversal* of the 'spirit' of discovery. This is the philosophical and, therefore, the theological capture and ensnaring of new phenomena, reducing them to conceptual structures of philosophy and institutional norms. The second, seemingly another version of the first, but in its objective appearance alone, is a *real inversion that is imposed or forced by a discovery in a given field of reception and respective hierarchies –* that is, a transformation or mutation of a field. While the reversal of the idealized and normalized field incorporates and dissolves the new phenomena of the Real into philosophical presuppositions, an inversion is communicated to this very same field in order to produce the being-identical of the Real. Indeed, this is less an inversion, though still an operation, than an assumption of the discovery or, put another way, the Real as the Inverse of the coded space of reception. Man-in-Person – in this context, Christ – is the Inverse as the very Identity of the theologico-philosophical Christian.

Yet St Paul receives Christ within a philosophical and Greek context, pushing him to divide unilateral identity or the lived of life and death and, furthermore, isolate this element and found it upon a supposed new life. The Pauline universalism is a 'deathly' rebellion of the Resurrection *against* the Risen. Modern conformity to St Paul's broadly anti-Judaic reversal is astonishing. But St Paul *not* turning against his own people would have been even more surprising still. The apostle is so taken by his own religion that he can only make the message sound like a philosophical essence and a malediction or accusation against Jews, who, recall, St Paul tells us, 'do not please God'. Efforts to reproach St Paul for this distortion and seek a mediation – a miserable corrective discourse and real contortion from the point of Judeo-Christian co-existence – would signal a common sense and philosophical understanding of the duality. This duality, without dialectical synthesis, implies the unheard message and a kind of universalization that would need to remain outside the Church.

In virtue of its relative novelty, Christianity is a paradigmatic example of the creation of a new 'confession'. It will have only subverted, in part, the initial problem(s) of monotheism and turned, in the end, towards a new religion, competing with others. This is due to the fact that the symbolic force of Christ had been reduced, from the very beginning, to the historical Jesus, within the context of contemporary religious phenomena. The reduction of this force in St Paul's message cuts universality off from its most radical root, that is, from the individual, in its general essence, and allows itself to be too much in thrall to the power of the Church. It would look back, in a nostalgic manner, towards philosophical universalism – that is, a Catholicism – and wish to found a more purely philosophical Church this time. Christ as the Risen and St Paul now understood in a wholly different manner: *St Paul according to Christ or understood starting from Christ this time, rather than the inverse.* This would be the truest duality, namely a confession *within the limits of* the Risen. The empirical, and, therefore, philosophical, reduction would sooner or later fall into an antinomy, opposing the catholicity of the Roman Church to the subjective life of the individual – either pietist or haughty and aristocratic – eventually leading to the scorning of the World, Jews, pagans, 'nations', and so forth, for the benefit of individual faith alone. In both cases, the foundation that engenders this duality between catholicity and individuality leads back to the presupposition that the announcement of the Risen in the Gospels is a milieu supposed either full of a religion that the new faith must complete without consummating it or empty of religion that the new faith must consummate without completing it. The antithetical relation between residual Roman paganism and the modern individualism of subjective faith, Church and sect, rests upon an objective appearance created by the confusion of faith and belief. In reality, the situation is more complex: the new life announced is *foreclosed precisely to the religion that provides the context and milieu for this announcement and forms the material to be transformed by it, rather than denied or prolonged*. It is, indeed, remarkable that the 'Christian' confession – we maintain this formula insofar as it does not 'turn' towards religion – only needs two fundamental factors, which are at the same time inseparable and heterogeneous within a genuinely unilateral mode, in order to produce salvation; and, if it does need a third term, then this would be contingent, occasional, carrying a transformed, non-dialectical sense. The religious triads or trinities have hitherto been organized in accordance with the function of God, not Man, belief, not faith. They are the symptoms of the transformation of confession in religion and must now be dualyzed. We pose (1) the primacy of faith over religion, (2) the primacy of faith over confession, and (3) the primacy of confession over religion. The non-standard order: faith, confession, then religion.

The inverse of Christianity

St Paul marks the birth of Christianity under, first of all, the form of a weakening of religion, like the Torah. But this is precisely only a weakening, rather than a change of terrain, even less a complete abandonment of this terrain. In order to accomplish the abandonment of every terrain and, above all, the terrain of the 'Whole' or 'All', a radical inversion of religion for the benefit of the Man-in-Person and faith – that is, a *faith without object*, and so without transcendence – must be posed. But this needs to be *accompanied*, on the religious side, by a simple transcendence. A paradoxical effect of St Paul's weakening of religion is the way this prepares us, following Christ, for a 'performed' or 'performative' abandonment – that is, a decision – of every inhuman and pre-human religion as well as allow us – we, the without-religion – to move towards 'the' religion, and, then, the non-religious.

St Paul opposes, for better or worse, the risen Christ to Judaism, universal salvation to the ancient religion, exemplified by the Mosaic law. The apostle does not, therefore, leave the sphere of religion. St Paul remains firmly within the religious sphere. This is all the more evident given that the Son of Man is recognized and understood to be the Son of God, through an act of transcendent affirmation, which follows from an unavoidable divine elevation and bedazzlement. It is a symptom of the Greco-philosophical context for the reception or revelation of Jesus. What St Paul sets in motion is a global reversal of the logic of religion in the name of a justification by faith. Yet faith is justice in-Person and does not justify Man but rather the world of religion. It is faith that either justifies or transforms the Law; it is faith that permits an exit from religion.

Human faith does not lack anything, not even the transcendence that does not belong to it. There is no need to institute this faith by circumcision – the price for God's power – that subjects man to the trace of the divine and testifies to man's election. A great step is taken when St Paul frees man from circumcision, even if this step is idealized and spiritualized in and through faith. But a second step completes this emancipation, passing through the abandonment of the most ideal and spiritual circumcision. Man is in-Man or in-Person, rather than emerging through an alliance with God or even with himself (the over-man or inter-human). Man-in-Man subtracts himself from any and every alliance with transcendence and tolerates only a unilateral relation with the world. The Immanent or the Undivided can, indeed, be an indivi-*dual*. But this does not mean it is comprised of two terms: the individual and the generic universal that accompanies it. There is no trace of synthesis or reduction. The generic plane of the non-religious contains two components seen from only one point of view. But from the perspective or mode of in-Man, Man is undivided with itself as One. Man is a Two that has never been unified, re-unified, or synthesized, owing to this aforementioned indivision in-One. It is essential to note and maintain the duality of Man (of) faith and religion, on one side, and a transformed – or even reformed – religion, on the other, throughout all preceding and subsequent discussions.

Such a Pauline rupture or reversal, operated still within the sphere of transcendence, leaves faith in an ambiguous situation. The Pauline mutation is incomplete. Only a generic decision, issuing from faith – that is, a radical and undivided rupture – can lead Christianity to its end, *eschaton*, and ultimatum. *Christ does not need to be received in a revelation; He is given by Man-in-Person and set once again under the form of faith; He comes before the world that He loved, first and above all, in order to deprive this same world of its sufficiency.* The world must receive Christ like the sword's edge or a *coup de grâce* – a great cleft.

The question of the 'end of religion' is as crucial as the problem of the 'end of philosophy' and requires the same kind of solution: an inversion rather than a reversal. Through an inversion, faith can set itself up as the generic essence of religion, while remaining completely foreclosed to it. Faith must be radicalized in order to be able to justify religion and its works; it can no longer be simply opposed to the theologico-institutional structures of religion (Luther). Faith is no more 'interior' than the orders of belief and the structures of the Church. The important task now concerns unification, without synthesis or relation, according to a unilateral duality – that is, a faith-without-religion and minus its theologico-religious milieu. This is precisely what the generic plane brings: the unification of faith and religion under the form of a duality that arises through a faith absent from any relation. What we seek here is a generic Catholicism rather than a Roman one; indeed, what is sought is a universality that could well provide a genuine phenomenal content to ecumenism; in short, it is a possible reduction of the *catholicitas*. The non-religious would be religious only insofar as it remains not in relation but 'in-accord' with and through faith. Religions reverse the problem and ask, instead, that the subject ensures their faith conforms, not so much to their works, actions, and deeds, but its particular structures.

Christ as immanent mediation or medium-without-mediation

A materialist and anti-philosophical interpretation, whether applied to St Paul or not, requires the immediate affirmation of the event or supernumerary *dictum*, along with the refusal of mediation. On this interpretation, the latter (mediation) is identified with knowledge and, in some sense, supposes an idealism, admitting that this always forms or constitutes a system. But mediation, if considered not to form part of an *ordo cognoscendi* in this way, stands effectively impotent in relation to this whole affair, arising, instead, from an *a priori* – that is, from a 'being-given' within an immanent Logos and Law, reduced to materiality. What prepares the ground for the coming of the historical Christ is precisely the non-paternal immanence of the Son, with the Subject standing as mediation, thereby offering to the world the suspension or impasse of religion. 'For St Paul, by contrast, just as for those who think a revolution is a self-sufficient sequence of political truth, Christ is a coming [*une venue*].'[1] We could not put this better ourselves, except by adding that Christ is not in Himself a 'self-sufficient' advent. Christ is like Man-in-Person in this respect, that is, arriving by means of futurality. Christ comes in a messianic manner, adding the dimension of Man-in-Person to the Subject. On the one hand, a Christian voluntarism is affirmed against any legislative function or wisdom that takes us back to philosophy, understood as auto-sufficient, without a single blow being made. But, on the other hand, given that 'paternity' is not completely annihilated, ever revealing the Principle of Sufficient Paternity, but rather transmutes this into a non-paternity without-sufficiency and that Christ is taken for the Son of Man, rather than God, it is possible and, indeed, necessary to distinguish between the futurality of Man as non-Father and the messianity of the Son, who, however, is only the subjective existence of futurality. Futurality is the universal *a priori* that Man-in-Person emits, without, importantly, 'existing' and messianity is the existence of the Subject-in-Struggle who 'overturns mountains'. The idealist error with respect to materialism can be found in the belief that 'the idea of mediation remains legal'.[2] This is a purely philosophical prejudice. On the contrary, only the *a priori* illegal, in radical immanence, grants legality and renders wisdom, commandment, and law illegitimate.

Mediation alone, above all if this remains in immanence and does not represent an exit from itself, can give rise to a practice. The Real is neither of the order of Being, Event, Decision, Cut, nor Memory. Doubtless, the Real has become in contemporary thought all these things. But for those with a passion for the new, it is a chance for a new decisive Subject that puts an end to the 'paradigmaticism' that annuls, in advance, any new emergence, through copies and simulacra, like a prophetism responsible for an exception. Only the content-of-the-real of the new, not formal eventality, can tear us most radically from the world. Good fortune alone, nothing more, can accomplish this rupture, since Christ is immediately inscribed within the horizon of Greek presuppositions with respect to the Logos or sometimes re-inscribed into those concerning the Torah through transcendence or a 'Christian logic' (Hegel). It is not enough to diagonalize (Badiou) Greek and Jewish discourse in order to oppose their synthesis. A diagonal is still a kind of transcendence; it is not the immanent unilaterality that suffuses and innervates discourse on the Son. Opposite St Paul's interpretation of Christ and the privilege given to the event and the operation of the Resurrection, we pose the Risen person such as He determines them as symptoms of an Identity without being – that is, an Identity that neither is nor is not and subtends the world.

Life and death are not easily verifiable, Resurrection even less so. But what is incommensurable with history and knowledge, even with the Resurrection, is less the idealist-materialist way in which this event is named and idealized than the Risen-without-Resurrection, the Subject-without-Subjection, the Insurgent – once and each time – that arrives in the world for the first time. We do not conclude from this, however, that the Resurrection is only a fable about a miracle and that the only decisive matter here would be its affirmation over and above everything else. The unrepentant theoreticism of the Pauline (anti-)philosophy lurks in the background once again, contemplating the decision to nominate or name this event. In much the same way Levinas invents an idle responsibility, without practice, Badiou, too, invents an idle decision about St Paul – an account of the event that is even more sterile than the one Deleuze puts forward. An invention by rupture and a will to universalism, without relation to diverse 'legalities', can certainly have the *effect* of universalism but cannot call itself a 'practice' insofar as it only contemplates effects and their excess. It is hardly surprising that the most theoretical philosophers compensate for this lack of any programme for work –that is, any practice – through a discourse on an 'excess of declaration' and the 'declaration of excess' (an *hubris*, beyond the hyperbole of the essence, i.e. apophatic theology, an excess of supernumerary nomination); the pathos of effects, a guerrilla war or skirmish, always stands close to the greatest violence and cannot ground a universalism. More so even than the Glorious Lived, the Glorious Infinite places the transcendence of the Logos or of the Torah in an impasse: the Risen is non-reason, without being irrational – the practice saves it – and non-sign, without being ineffable – the practice is the transformation of the world as a discursive link. The Lived-Christ bears witness to Man, not the man of Being, the Other, *anthropos*, or any other philosophical and theological determination.

The revindication of the sole event of nomination as 'a completely precarious having-taken-place',[3] in rejecting both the logos and prophetic signs, not only carries the risk of seeming arbitrary, where the subject is understood to decide the event retroactively, but also does not prevent any return to transcendence or duality of the finite-infinite – that is, to the philosophico-religious that sub-tends this kind of decision. Nothing guarantees that the 'truths' that suppose this philosophy of the event may be 'truths' in this sense. They may, indeed, really be arbitrary. No precarity can assure itself of its own precariousness, even if this leads back to uncertainty or the *precarious certainty* of philosophy. This duality rests upon the subject. The subject supports truth through the material conditions of its immanence or the site for the truths it generates. But immanence can only be a *spiritual* materiality and 'truths' can arise only from the acts of the Subject, not at all from the action of Ideas moving in the void. The subject only has half-proofs or, more precisely, occasions for such decision, which, by definition, are not foundations. They are, instead, declarations or axioms. But the form of such decisions is determined by the Real, that is, Man, not the Subject.

The philosophico-religious sphere is occupied by 'discourses' that are mixed by syntheses that are factors of consensus or social link. The two initial philosophico-religious discourses are Greek and Jewish, the Logos and the Propheme. But philosophy has encountered two other discourses that should not be underestimated with respect to their development and complication, that is, Catholic dogma or the forceful discourses of Authority and reformed Scripture or the weak discourse of Democracy. It is strange that philosophers carry on as though such discourses did not exist, not even acknowledging their sedimented effects in modernity and quite often receiving them as evident or combined at best, two by two, upon the basis of a supposed priority of the Greek discourse. Whether Christianity has been, at the origin, a 'discourse', that is, a social link, a factor of consensus remains uncertain. But this certainly became St Paul's impulse in order subsequently to set out with some difficulty a 'dramatics of reconciliation' (dogma/heresy, Church/schism, reform/counter-reform, sectarian pluralism). A contemporary reflection upon this needs to be founded once again, predominantly philosophical or even theological, not only upon two of these discourses (Greek and Roman, Jewish and Reformed, Greek and Jewish, Roman and Reformed), that is, contemplation of an abusive primacy or dominant exception, but rather the entire set or *quadripartite*, without, perhaps, forgetting their sectarian multiplication. Philosophy needs religious phenomena precisely for two reasons: first of all, as an index of the Real and, in the end, the reality or object that philosophy treats, then, secondly, as a form of discourse according to the Real. With respect to the Real, religious phenomena are equally decisive for non-philosophy, as much as the Greek discourse and the Transcendentals (the Beautiful, the Good, and so on), touching upon the divine in philosophical reflection, as the Jews, with the affect of the infinite, as Christianity, with the reduction of God to a mediation through Christ, and, finally, as the Reformation, with the practice of faith. But they are each decisive for different reasons. What matters here is the deduction of the form of the Word that follows from the Real. Dogma thus becomes an authoritarian symptom of this thesis, even a philosophical axiom. Scripture transforms into a quasi-algorithm that produces an external mathematization of a philosophical mystery. The Propheme turns into the 'text-to-come' and Rabbinic interpretation becomes the practical exercise of messiah-fiction and, therefore, philo-fiction, the Logos as transcendental sense of the concept.

Subjects can sustain numerous divisions beyond the distinction between the Greek and Jew. Philosophy tends to set down a single type of division or decision – bi-lateral or reversible in-the-last-instance – among humans and conceives the religious on this model. This division of subjects traverses the entirety of philosophy.

Our 'militantism' is, in the end, disabused of any Christian apologetics. There is no one, no atheist, no nation to convince, nothing to prove in order to believe and know, and, above all, no non-Christianity that is more 'true' than Christianity, rather a non-true that is its entire truth. This means that all Humans are always and already messiahs and, so, do not need to become so. If the Good News were not, from the start, good or 'new', then what would such news serve, if not to give a task or mission to priests and theologians? The faithful are not scholars, though not at all deprived of an 'unlearnt' knowledge; rather, fidelity determines scholars as Subjects.

Messianity as sub-version of Christianity

There are two versions of a well-known thesis, half-historical and half-philosophical, each verifying the other, concerning the 'axial' character of Christianity in the Western tradition. The claim that Christianity and philosophy sustain between themselves a speculative relation is precisely what Hegel and later Deconstruction suppose according to certain speculative undecidables, with one sometimes forming the model for the constitution of the other. The identity and history of Christianity is seen as self-surpassing. It matters little the way in which these interpretations overlap one another. We receive them simply as symptoms to dualyze. The problem begins beyond this half-historical and half-philosophical thesis. The axial character indicates an orientation, an evident exterior teleology, but wholly interior to Christianity. There is, indeed, a certain self-surpassing of Christianity. But such a thesis can only have any sense and find formulation in terms of a philosophical overcoming or sublation. Where does this tend and what does it realize? This thesis depends upon another, more radical one that founds not only contemporary post-Kantian thought but philosophy in general, by means of history and empirical evidence, namely the *primacy of immanentization over immanence, finality over the end (of Christianity), the Christian operation over the real knot of Christianity*. There are two versions of this teleology or making immanent of Christianity. The first – the version in a 'major' key – signifies in general that Christianity accomplishes, fulfils, and then dies in order to be born to itself, and, moreover, it has never announced anything other than its own end under the form of a divine presence. But, more broadly, Christianity carries within its own self-surpassing the death of all religions; it represents an 'exit' from the religious – that is, an end of religions much like the supposed 'exit' from philosophy in order for thought to begin again otherwise (Heidegger). Without doubt, the Christian message is time, that is, 'the concept of time' (Hegel), but also that the message needs time, that is, transcendence; the end of time needs temporality and remains inseparable from history. The second – the version now in a 'minor' or 'minoritarian' key, even the repressed one – is called 'gnosticism' and signifies, more politically, that this immanentization of the Christian *telos* amounts to the loss of transcendence and the meaning of truth, through which the soul, in the Greek sense, holds in itself, for the benefit of the will to power, universal domination, destroying all transcendence – for example, the gnosticism of Ernst Vögelin. Let us set to one side the historical and philosophical relevance this political, albeit somewhat simplified, interpretation of gnosis has for the present discussion. This is worth less in itself than an insistent comparison with the major or dominant interpretation(s) that leave it undecidable, crossing one another in the works of Hegel, Marx, and Nietzsche. This minoritarian branch, historically and dogmatically repressed by the constitution of the 'Roman Leviathan', can be called 'anti-Christianity' in many senses, with allusions to the Anti-Christ, if you like. Above all, it stands parallel to an 'anti-philosophy, (Lacan) that accompanies philosophy like a transversal or a diagonal (Badiou). Christianity does not prevail only through such accomplishments or arise from itself like an absolute or divine spirit but also arises just as much from the black and dangerous form that accompanies it, namely, the clandestine form of the triumphant gnostic over-man.

Both versions do not interest us so much for their supposed truth, only for the symptoms each brings in relation to our present undertaking. What is necessary here is not so much their 'analysis' than their dualysis. Dualysis is the inverse of analysis: the gnostic interpretation is first, the classical Christian one comes second; the latter must submit to a gnostic deconstruction for the benefit of the immanentization of Christianity in the (over)man. In reality, the thesis that poses the priority of gnostic immanentization over and above orthodox Christianity finds itself subordinate to another thesis: the primacy of the non-gnosticism of Man over the religious – that is, the 'Son of Man' over God. This marks the priority of *another, more radical immanence over immanentization*. The Son of Man is this ultimatum, that is, the last term, rather than the prior thesis cast against Christianity, and, therefore, cast against all religions, in order not only to accomplish and complete itself (this is the symptom of the Christian end of religion) but also to recognize, for better or worse, the primacy of Christ-in-Person over the primacy of the historical Christ. Indeed, it concerns very much Christ-the-Gnostic, in His radical immanence. But this immanence is an immanence-without-telos, annihilating any sense of finality and thereby transforming all teleology. Rather than oppose once again gnosticism to orthodox Christianity for the greatest benefit of the Church, that is, to continue the anti-heretical combat by bringing this to the political plane, the more radical thesis initiates the reversal of teleological immanentization, and, more profoundly, turns the arrow of *telos*, travelling from the past to the future, the other way; it now travels from the future towards the past. But this reversal, more profoundly still, transforms the arrow itself, taking away any direction or sense from it – that is, any *di*-rection or bilaterality that would otherwise determine its course; it is now rection as unilateral, that is, rection as unirection. The movement of this goes from immanence, such as Man assumes it, towards the Son of Man-in-Person. It sub-verts Christianity quite literally, almost without any more metaphor than can be found in the formula 'Son of Man'. What do we mean by 'literal subversion'? Man-in-Person, without being subtracted from the (philosophical) insult 'rational animal' or proceeding by way of a retreat or a withdrawal, 'sub-tends' the foundation of radical immanence under the form of an *a priori* messianity. This offers the Christian-world, but only by 'turning' it outside itself, that is, from out of its historical and religious 'self'. The sub-tension of Man amounts to a 'sub-turning' that renders immanence accessible through turning, rather than reversing. The *version* of Christianity by Man is a simple *version*, not a re-versal or re-version, like the philosophers say (from Eckhart to Deleuze). Christianity will be the symptom of the last religion. It is thus necessary to identify this ultimate character in terms of the 'last instance', that is, the 'sub-turning' of Man into the Son of Man. The Messiah has His own way of remembering God or His Father, as certain Russian mystics say. It is the Father – here the Man-in-Person – who 'sub-tends' as an *a priori* of the Son, Archi-Son or Archi-Christ. The Father clones the Son in the form of a subject, starting from the *a priori* furnished to Him by the Christ-world. Christianity is the immanent operative method that emerges from Man-in-Person in order to transform the history-world and, above all, the religion(s)-world. There is no longer any historico-religious consideration; they would found nothing save sufficient and deathly claims (see above). The real content of Christianity is a radial immanentization of this process. We understand Christianity as the symptom of an operative method that is strictly human in its cause, subjective in its effectivity, and destined to struggle against the (re-)doubled attachment, ever re-affirming itself, of the subject to the religion-world. This has nothing to do with a deconstruction of Christianity (Nancy), anticipating and undermining itself through a more or less 'differed' or 'deferred' term or end; rather, it is a radically immanent deconstruction and, therefore, heteronomous in virtue of its wholly fictitious inscription within an Outside, namely, the Future, that contains nothing essential, only an occasional content. Deconstruction allows itself to be limited by the presuppositions of the philosophical tradition and only operates upon Christianity by still recognizing itself as Christianity, and, ultimately, as Christian. What distinguishes the last remaining operations of philosophy upon itself, from the ultimatum practice of non-Christianity? What is this 'last thing' set in advance? We distinguish the ultimate, understood as the remaining philosophical operation(s), from the non-philosophical ultimatum that determines such philosophical operations and makes them into its simple material that 'seems' to be a remainder that hallucinates philosophy with blind eyes. It is precisely due to the fact that we do not set 'in advance' this last thing – that is, Man-in-Person – that the Real possesses a primacy, not a priority, which would claim to count the Real and order it within the calculus of a first or second philosophy, even to a 'Whole' or 'All'. On the contrary, the (non-philosophical) ultimatum or the 'last instance' determines what is first or what 'sub-tends' as the *a priori* first that cannot be identified with itself. The Real sets down an ultimatum to the world but does so only for the world, which, by contrast, sees this only as a remainder or remnant. This is the radical misunderstanding of hallucination.

In the same way, we may ask: what distinguishes the negation of Christianity in deconstruction and non-Christianity (in messianity)? The deconstruction of Christianity employs not the negation of negation but rather a 'soft' or 'gentle' negation, via an alterity, that is measured against logo-centric non-being; furthermore, it is complex, doubled, relative, and otherwise absolute. Non-Christianity deduces rather the non- from the One-in-One, that is, an *a priori* non-One, rather than from a non-being, and so remains immanent, affecting the whole of philosophy as such through what arises from it. The absolute death of Christianity in terms of the Resurrection, that is, through self-surpassing, produces an un- or over-Christianization that rests upon pious, philosophical wishes, which are not lacking in efficacy. But all this amounts to a series of symptoms for a Christo-dualysis, which must be set within the humanity of Christ, rather than at the centre of an over-arching paradigm or structure. This delegates or 'missions' Man as an organon or instrument. What changes here is the function of mediation. Neither idealist auto-mediation nor materialist refusal of mediation, the transformed mediation here marks the primacy of medium-without-mediation that is wholly immanent and, therefore, *a priori*. The cloned subjects, standing at the limits of Humanity, are messianic organons of the last struggle against the worldly and mundane, and signify that Man-in-Person is the radical transcendental or the Real, determining this work of messianity. Born-Strangers to all religion and in conflict with a world-horizon that ceaselessly takes flight in order only to re-envelop the world with greater insistence, we have the hope of solitude. This is how we honour the event of Christianity: by being Christs, rather than Christians. We re-situate the historical 'over-coming' of Christianity, stranger to the milieu of religions, through the 'sub-tending' of a messianity, stranger to Christianity itself. Man himself is without-message. There is nothing to announce. What Man needs is a subject, more than a preacher of a message, who would confuse himself or herself with it. At the level of non-Christianity, we call 'subjects' the Messengers, who are, indeed, identical to the Message made and given in the world and the religion-world. Such Messengers are sent from Nowhere – that is, from Man. The 'end' announced by Christianity is the symptom of the Real as 'last thing', dedicated to the announcement of a radical delay – a delay of anticipation that is always the Word. This radical delay of any and every anticipation forms kerygma fiction. We may, indeed, be Strangers to Christianity, without being anti-Christs – for an anti-Christianity means only one thing – but the historical Christ, the religion, confessions, and churches that result from Him are models for us, the Future Christs. Christianity and the Gospels are a model for non-Christianity.

On the plane of salvation, we make a *tabula rasa*

What is this plane of salvation – this history planned by God, combining creation, sin, redemption, and the last judgement – that takes the Human for its object? How does this salvation phenomenologically manifest itself? A theological form of philosophical *parousia* – a final advent of God – is needed, offering the full presence of the divine to men in the form of a second and 'last' revelation, mediated for the first time by Christ and the Incarnation. But the need for a second revelation after Christ – that is, the second coming – is incomprehensible, or even too comprehensible, if only for reasons regarding transcendence or philosophy. Transcendence always demands that an event repeats itself, that it doubles itself. This is precisely the point where philosophico-theological duplicity reveals itself. The history of salvation is only a torsion to which religion, in particular Christianity, submits only through a division, via transcendence, and extension into the historico-celestial space of history. Even the thesis that a supernumerary event draws from its conditions or its situation the power to name – that is, the thought that narrows its own limits and idealises an event through the power of nomination (e.g. the nomination of the 'Resurrection' by St Paul according to Badiou) – carries, perhaps, the last remnant of this philosophical duplicity. The thesis that there is a divine history of salvation can thus be understood to be the simple projection into an hallucinated transcendence, across which, in reality, passes Man-in-Person, who 'missions' or clones the subject. There is only a *parousia* that has always already taken place. This is the eternity of salvation that renders churches useless. If Christ has, indeed, come, then even religions that believe in His return – that is, as Christ, subject-in-person –, need only this single 'sub-tending', once and for the first time, in order to ensure us of salvation. There will be no return of Christ (against all sects and their phantasms of the return or second coming). The plane of salvation, like any programme, even a 'plane of immanence' (Deleuze), inscribed in transcendence and postulating a projected future starting from the past or present, is the deception and distortion of Man-in-Person by transcendence.

The sole and scarcely concrete content of the plane of salvation that can be apperceived is not an impossible levelling but rather the extinction of the Church. Such a claim rests upon the fact that the *tabula rasa* here indicates the void that 'sub-tends' the Church as much as Man. This places the Church under an immanent condition and prepares the way for its consummation by subjects. The problem of the extinction of the Church runs parallel to the question of the extinction of the State. But this parallel is much less apparent given that the Church has not yet had its own Karl Marx, only a few Marxists, who grasps religion only from an external perspective as an 'ideological apparatus'. Yet, if one sees within this plane a philosophical schema, then the plane of salvation arranges, in a very general and classical manner, the extinction of the Church through the final revelation of God. It would be interesting to pose the problem of a post-ecclesial 'exit' and the 'end' of the Church *as well as* religion, alongside a parallel departure out from philosophy. But the essential is, for now at least, to agree upon this extinction. It cannot be an empirical concept, that is, a philosophico-religious one. There will be no confusion between their avatars or their decline with a rigorous concept, namely Man, who 'sub-tends' in-Person and orders, without condition, this extinction, thus turning it into a symptom. Projected into the space of history and transcendence, and supposed effective, extinction is evidently a myth that both Church and State can only triumphantly resist. But if this is understood in accordance with radical immanence, then the state is already extinguished in Man, who is not a political animal; furthermore, the Church is eternally extinguished – more than consummated and even consumed – in Man, who is not a religious animal. The 'sub-tending' of subjects beneath the State and the Church is, moreover, precisely what sets the latter under a condition and a transformation. Subjects are determined precisely by means of their being in-Struggle *with*, not *for*, State and Church; they are rendered impossible or set in impasse in order to produce a political-fiction and a religion-fiction that transforms current, effective political regimes and religions into a model.

Humans have some right to suspect a 'plane of salvation' that owes nothing to their own work of transforming the world but, instead, solely and completely upon their repentance. This is the equivalent of a theoreticism or contemplation put within the reach of many Christians by philosophers, who, for example, contemplate the 'courage' and 'ascesis' of truth. Bad consciousness, consciousness of the fall, repentance, and so forth, demands a subject, but a subject who contemplates Evil with some nuances like another subject contemplating truth or wisdom. If the focus concerns a struggle against Evil, then Man-in-Person alone, not the subject, must identify it in an axiomatic way in order to decide *wisely or knowingly the cause* of its essence. But this does not mean that Evil is unfathomable or 'inscrutable' for thought; on the contrary, only Humans can decide Evil as an indestructible structure of the World in the very same gesture that subjects are distinguished from it. It is difficult not to see a complacent and lazy contemplation upon truth with respect to original sin that affects the subject. One will not simply oppose work to contemplation, which is always practical and laborious in its own way, even less so to the tortures of repentance; rather, what matters here concerns the problem of identity, not the generality or the worldly universality of work. Philosophers and theologians distribute work between God and men, between philosophers and priests; they make subjects irresponsible and thereby condemn them much more assuredly to a bad, dangerous complacency, and an evil that affects them without hope of salvation, barring some last-minute miracle. Salvation must be entrusted to all the possible labours and works of Humans alone, along with their subjects, much like Levinas. With the thesis of an absolute responsibility of the subject, Levinas is close to entrusting the task of the transformation of the world to them. But given that this is a passive responsibility, through and through, and, moreover, forced by the Other or God, Levinas moves completely away from it. What matters here concerns less a worldly generality of work than a *uniq*ue distinction of human subjects from the general form of the world: a world-form that is lived and given in its identity, once and each time, as well as a transformation of the very identity of the world. The subject is subject (of) Man-in-Person, not at all subject to the 'Other man'.

The disciple and the apostle: A dualysis of the apostolic tradition

We will not allow ourselves to forget the famous 'omnipotence' of 'priests' under the pretext of being an 'antiquity' that contemporaries, with an air of understanding, complacency, and gluttony, say has been 'surpassed' in some way. The struggle against the priests of total obedience and the objective ignorance propagated by them is never 'overcome', no more than religion itself, and its activity, which resides in the order of 'forcing' and propaganda. If, for example, creationism made a return, like any ideology almost anywhere (and sooner than Christ will ever make His return …), with the sharpest arguments, then this struggle against voluntary ignorance would become urgent and could be done now in the name of a more elaborated faith in the context of an *a priori* defence of Man against religions. From this point of view, a 'dualysis' of the 'apostolic tradition' – a central pillar of the Roman Church that permits judgement concerning the possibility for certain Christian confessions of faith to 'make a return' or not into the fold of the Church – becomes necessary. One ordinarily distinguishes, for the purpose of simplification, the historically continuous tradition that the Roman Church claims for itself from the Apostolic line that this same Church 'relates' and 'gathers' to itself. But the Apostolic relation constitutes another nature altogether, not historical, and another faith, more spiritual, within which certain confessions would be content. Aside from certain questions concerning legitimacy, other than those posed with a mixture of violence and crime, that history could bring to this debate – an ideologically self-legitimizing violence, following, like an applied discipline, the production of the visible body of Christ – it is now a convenient time to return once more to the philosophical foundation of this distinction and the origins of its Greco-Papist usage. It may, perhaps, be necessary to choose between a 'disciple' of Jesus and a 'disciple' of St Paul …

Let us return once again to the founder of Christianity, namely the intermediary between Christ the Gnostic – the 'non-'Jewish – and St Peter the legislator for the new State. St Paul did not really see Christ nor directly receive the message of life but will, however, see and receive both in a quasi-, almost Greek, mode of illuminating revelation, neither Jewish nor Christian, on the road to Damascus. This event comes to determine the destiny of Christianity. St Paul founds his mission entirely upon a life and message much more abstract, upon a lived experience, certainly, but a secondary or derivative one, namely upon Christ risen among the dead, sublimated and idealized afterwards, despite everything. Whence, having not been a disciple, St Paul was constrained to proclaim himself an apostle – a disciple after death. This changed the very nature of faith *demanded or called* by Christ by giving, as the object of faith, belief in the theoretical primacy of the Resurrection over the Risen. Put in our own idiom, the Pauline account gives the subject *par excellence*, the paradigmatic Father of the 'preacher' or 'priest' – that is, not the Man (of) faith reduced to immanence; it is the subject who, finding the confrontation with the world too much, is left bewitched and thinks Christ according to the function of a dialectical struggle that plays out in the world. The duality of the disciple, which is sufficiently described in a discourse of simplicity, with images, parables, miracles, and so forth, that characterizes the apostle's perspective, where a mission is assigned from the highest and the most distant, is decisive for an evaluation of the role in a way that is not historical or factual but rather constitutive precisely for philosophy in the Christian 'turning'. A distinction must be made between the first apostles and later ones, like St Paul, who are already, in some sense, conquered by the world, victims of all the ambiguities there, and, sadly, endowed with the means to spread them. But this distinction must not be made in a doctrinaire fashion. We are not saying that the first apostles are naïve disciples, penetrated by faith alone. As we have already suggested, the famous apostolic tradition is, in reality, already *differing* or *deferred* and permits every subsequent interpretation, dogmatic interpolation, and their 'development'. There is not a single individual or Church able to claim ownership of this tradition. Even the Man (of) faith is not the proprietor of himself and, above all, not 'his' faith. The work of faith takes shape in the struggle against the Principle of Sufficient Catholicism, namely the

Roman Church, and, in general, against every other minor form and variation: confessions structured in accordance with hierarchical institutions, through consecration or privilege, ministry or the Good. We leave to one side sects, whose hierarchy is structured around sex, money, and the weakness of belief – this is the negative or reverse side of the Church. The only tradition *in real time* is the clonage by faith of a faithful subject and the primacy of the Risen over the Resurrection. This is the real content of the apostolic tradition insofar as it does not find itself confused with or distorted by history. The phrase 'in-real-time' does not necessarily indicate a simultaneity, a presence, or even synchrony. The Real of time is the ur-chronic future, that is, the temporality of the Messiah but only insofar as expected 'actually' to come or arrive as Performed, then decided by clonage.

The first disciple or apostle is in the image of Christ. Despite every shortcoming and hesitations, the first can be pardoned. Even Jesus is not exempt from hesitations. Regardless, faith does not measure itself here against the unbreakable solidity of a *fundamentum inconcussum*; it is much more feeble and 'finite' than the Cogito, and much more universal. The disciple is limited by his or her religion of origin and the power of reception and territory of activity is compressed within this limit. But faith shines immediately, *even if it is only a blinking or flickering light, scintillating in a hesitant manner*, and is not at all systematic or doctrinal. This faith is a lived utopia, walking in the footsteps of Jesus on the outskirts of Jerusalem. But this utopia remains misunderstood; it lacks any extension, since the world is not its object. On the contrary, it is a content ready and waiting to come into the world. No longer capable of comprehension and unable to be enveloped or gathered into itself, faith can only emit parables and exhortations, speaking in symbols, which are always real axioms. Such incomprehensible axioms are *realized* prophesies, rather than real – that is, *performed* – without being extended throughout the world.

As for the apostle, who is not, first of all, a disciple, he, too, is Man (of) faith, but under the paradigmatic and, therefore, somewhat secretly Greek form of St Paul. The subject is represented by means of reflection and the organon soon becomes a braced and ready arm, cloned by the Man (of) faith, certainly, but starting this time from religious structures. This means that the subject takes himself into the world, which, consequently, forms now the sole field of practice. The subject acts within the network of relations that constitute the struggle with the world of religion, that is, the Gentiles and the Nations, even Israel. Distinct from the disciple, called in *the image of Jesus and no longer the image of God*, we understand the apostle much more clearly now as the clone of the priest or man of religion, that is, a clone determined by faith, which alone has the force to tear a subject from religion. The clone is the subject insofar as without-relation (to the World) but nevertheless enters into a quasi-relation with religion and the religion-world. This is what we call the 'being-in-donation' or 'being-in-concurrence' of religion that has been transformed by and in terms of the subject. The apostle is the subject insofar as struggling with the world through fidelity or faith. But from this struggle an apostle or subject can be seduced by the religion-world that he or she will have 'forgotten' to transform.

The *a priori* defence of faith by the paraclete

Should the Church be forgiven? Does the State receive our pardon? No, we cannot accord any pardon to them. Religions are in general unforgivable, like the world. The only real problem is how to save them as much as possible, that is, how to gather together and complete them, even consummate them. This would call both State and Church to the status of the Risen. The Church, understood as a visible and surviving body, especially needs salvation – the real content of forgiveness.

The generic conception of faith simplifies the structure of the triadic system that makes up the Trinity and 'reverses' its function. Under the form of a unilateral duality (faith/religion, faith/belief, faith/generic belief), the triadic structure of the Trinity acquires a new function, passing now from an apparatus for oppression by the Church towards the state of an *a priori* defence of the faithful subject. The Father and Son are not the only terms to be reversed and upset within the Trinitarian economy in such a way that the Son becomes radically autonomous, without taking the place of the Father, and sends Him (the Father) back towards the world or His transcendent surroundings. Does the Holy Spirit, understood as a Person (hypostasis), still have any meaning? Dare we ask whether the Spirit has a future? Should it be maintained, given the persistent difficulties involved in associating this particularly indeterminate concept with the Father and the Son?

The Holy Spirit is sometimes called a paraclete, that is, an advocate. Alongside the faithful subject, as we understand this at least, stands the organon with respect to the Word of the Man (of) faith – even as an advocate. Perhaps a sense and necessary function could be found on this basis. The defence is less here the work of an external advocate or paraclete insofar as the three Persons of the Trinity are extrinsic to one another, than an immanent act that merges with the work of faith or salvation. The Resurrection that this advocate performs or operates through the world by way of consummatory consummation (i.e. the deployment of the destruction of sufficiency) constitutes the very defence of the Man (of) faith. There is no other defence, no other advocate, despite its various forms (theoretical, political, ecclesiological, and so on). The immanent paraclete is the subject itself understood as a faith 'missioned' via cloning. Like any advocate, the Holy Spirit defends *a priori* the one who missions but only assumes this on the basis that its 'cause' – that is, the 'case' – remains itself an *a priori* one. Even in the judicial sphere, the right to a defence is something inalienable or even an extra-judicial principle that is probably human insofar as Man 'assumes the right' or stands for the Real in law. What else could be asked from the Holy Spirit, understood as separated, even 'separated-without-separation' by the cause that directs it, than not to be the celebrated 'spokesperson' or 'representative' *ex machina* that always arises anonymously from philosophy? What more could we ask from the Spirit than simply to be the advocate for the defence of faith against the world?

Having thus become the immanent paraclete, directly missioned by faith for the defence, the faithful subject could also be just as much the subject bewitched by the magic of the world. But the subject does not assume each state for the same reason. The struggle against the world of religion is doubtless done with the help of religion (but remains itself only the occasion for fidelity) and always placed under the determination made by the fidelity of the subject.

3

Surviving scripture, glorious scripture

Incarnation as clonage

A transcendent entity, God, is schematized in the flesh in an equally transcendent manner – this is the Christian Incarnation. It is difficult to imagine no scriptural mediation here, forming thus a relation between the two terms ('God' and 'man') in such a schematization. Scripture is thus the third term. But the break from the imaginary alliance with Christian theology implies henceforth that Incarnation is no longer for God, but Man, through clonage, in the form-world-in-person, under the species of Christ-Subject, not the schematization of distinct terms. Non-Christianity is a theory of the production of subjects in terms of clonage. Subjects are the product of the Glorious Body, starting from the theologico-religious form of the world, taken as material and symptom. The Incarnation supposes the transcendence of the Real. But the primacy – if such terms are still permissible – accorded to the Glorious Body, which itself has no need to be incarnated, having lost any transcendence and thus separate from the world, implies a transformation of the two concepts: Incarnation and Resurrection. This involves, first of all, the abandonment of the philosophical exigence of scripture or writing, understood as the third-term for mediation. The Incarnation and Resurrection are now unilateral operations of the subject, and, consequently, immanent. The real content of these terms can be found in the assumption of the world by the Glorious Body, which 'missions' the Identity (of the World) in real time. The 'mission' of the Man (of) faith, unlike the fleshly schematization of God, is instant, without delay, owing to the unilateral transformation of the Incarnation and the Resurrection. But given that both terms lack mediation in order to ensure their transit, they are thus forced. Man passes in-force into the world or clones in-force the world. The faithful subject is a forced emergence that could not at all be foreseen. The world such as it is given in and for itself contains, however, many conceivable forms, ends, materials, and causes. But the simplicity of the world, that is, non-duplicity, arises from a *coup de grâce* that is immanent to such forms, completing them at the same time as being heteronomous to them.

There is no originary bilateral continuity, operated by the transcendental imagination (Kant), for example, or the contemporary equivalent, writing (Derrida), between Man, understood as universal *a priori* for the world, and the world, twisted and turned towards the human *a priori*, as if towards a hypostasis. Faith, understood precisely in terms of separation, intervenes in the world along with a certain concurrence with the world, making thus emerge something that has not had any chance hitherto to do so, if one had only considered the world with respect to itself alone. The miracle is that religion, philosophy, and everything else that contributes to the formation of the world find themselves turned inside-out by faith, leaving behind their supposed sufficiency, rather than the world being understood to arise from nothingness (*ex nihilo*), as certain creationist religions intend. They have invented, under this simple form, a non-religion or non-philosophy, brought about by faith at each moment. The world emerges outside from itself towards Man, through its effect, which is not at all to be understood in terms of Aristotle's prime mover. The Gospels give us an imperfect model for this birth or being-born without-birth. But the passage-in-force of the Man (of) faith, that is, the intervention in and upon the world, which is always given in terms of an object interior to itself, has been set outside itself, projected into the infernal sky of transcendence; it has thus become the schematization of the abstract in the concrete, a duplicitous and greco-religious form of faith.

In the end, we will give another meaning to the Last Supper, understood as a symbolic opening (in the sense of an anticipatory image) or even as a model of Christ. What has been called a *trans-substantiation* (resonating with our sense of 'trans-formation' on condition that this is understood in terms of the Glorious Body as the Christ-form) or sometimes a co-substantiation, in a rightly theological and Greek style, seems to be here, from a philosophical point of view, a de-substantiation. But this is not a complete or total de-substantiation; rather, what we will call an operation of *uni-substantiation* or even, ever in our own idiom, clonage as non-substantiation. Faith institutes this uni-substantiation, that is, the real phenomenal content of the Eucharist. The Logos loses its claim to incarnate the Real, which now takes refuge in faith, and finds itself reduced to a simplified and idealized body of Christ, set within the memory of the empty tomb. The theological story of Christianity is the hallucinatory re-substantiation and ontologico-religious falsification of the Glorious Body of Christ.

Should Christianity be deconstructed? Surviving scripture, surviving writing

The more God is unique and transcendent, the more the book and writing are the single, real support for monotheist religions and the very last mirror for this God. Before this God, voices are hushed, tending towards silence. Churches, more developed forms of sects, and sects, which are nothing but concentrated forms of the Church, are the natural product of monotheism just as the gods, mysteries, and multiple temples are for pagan religions. God, who proclaims himself unique, must accept the multiple or the many in some form or another. Sects are mono-sectarian by definition; churches are mono-ecclesial or ecclesiological by constitution and destination. Each and every form is the real, monadic point of view for the unique God. Opposition between the Church and sects is only ever justified locally, at a very small scale. The ruse committed by sects is precisely to take at face value the logic of monotheism and steer God towards contradiction. This God botched creation and theology bungled the thought of creation, since neither imposes univocity. The lack of this has turned creation into an object for philosophy and theology, dissolving creation into scripture or writing. As if the divine understanding did not cease to fall victim to an hallucination, reflected and admired in Man's eyes, which see this projection, like a giant phantasm, in a narcissistic soul. Before such an affront, arising solely from a careless theological fiction, the human, social, and historical conditions for the reception of God could be invoked. But none are at all pertinent beyond the occasional contingency of the history-world, which is only too evident, but nevertheless, in such objects, posed incorrectly in terms of a sufficient cause for the reception of God. Such facts have no meaning or use for us, except as models – the single important thing for the most radical logic of phenomena. This is the unicity of the transcendent God, determined in a reciprocal manner by the history-world and scripture (or writing). This is, at least, what philosophical logic imposes on each and every divine fantasy and daydream of height and oneness, which, in a more specifically religious context, can be understood and subjected to a certain criticism only on the basis of a philosophical foundation, granting them their intelligibility.

Between the one God and the human expressions that follow, between the One and the Multiple, there must, indeed, be a mediation in order to reconstitute a triad that philosophy could administer and operate. Within this 'monotheist' context, such a mediation and reconstitution is accomplished in the form of texts and 'books' that, in addition to their spontaneously fetishistic character, are reputed to be 'sacred' in some sense or other. The entire text is 'full' or 'suffuse' with significance; sacred objects and things not only exclude chance but also endow whatever sign is made with a meaningful intention. While laic or profane texts fill any gap in sense within the potential *con*-text of – that is, text-*with* – the world alone, under diverse forms (perception, history, and so on) and always ecstatic-horizontal, sacred texts fill them with an actual or present ecstatic-vertical intention, up to and including absence, more or less moving backwards according to the logic of monotheism. How does this triad, which founds the possibility for a spiritual hermeneutic of the world, function? This triad is a system of extases (God or His word, man or 'faith', and the text or meaning) that encroach upon one another in a circular fashion. It produces intelligence, namely faith, which, when examined closely, reveals precisely this mutual encroachment – that is, a perpetual sliding or slippage that troubles the soul, creating the sensation and desire for a transcendent interiority. But a faith produced in this manner is structurally duplicitous, that is, simply belief. This kind of 'faith' can, indeed, touch the Absolute, envelop God and the soul, and surpass the objects of belief. But it substitutes for such separated objects of belief a hesitation and uncertainty that contaminates its radicality.

Faith is, however, an ecstasis, re-enveloping itself, and thereby becoming infinite, dissolving into its own slippages. This is a unilateral structure, too finite to have an otherwise illusory 'knowledge' of itself, and directed, without hesitation, towards the form-world (religion), against which faith arrives as Stranger-in-Person. As soon as uniqueness and inalienability, formerly inscribed within the divine, are admitted as immanent and accepted as such, they change their course and Real mode of insertion. With Christ-in-Person, such univocity ruptures at the generic threshold of a non-theology in the form of a uni–voice – the really unique call, without either a caller or a respondent. This uni–voice is the ultimatum that forces me, as a speaking and writing subject. It is not God who is unique, but Man. Yet the unicity of Man is no longer numeric or transcendent; rather, Man is unique by being simply in-Man and the voice is unique by being simply in-voice. The heno-phonology signals the 'end' of authoritarian logocentric philosophy. Christianity warrants, indeed deserves, more than a deconstruction (Nancy), if it rests, like any philosophy, upon the reduction of scripture in general – sacred or profane – to *the factual-idealized existence of the signifying, doubtless re-worked and altered.* Christianity is only a text for the subject who believes in this far-too-narrow linguistico-Judaic presupposition and believes itself to be able to draw the former from the latter. This raises the following question: how to operate such a critique without, first of all, justifying the basis for doing so, that is, without asking whether this has given philosophy the means to surpass its own ontologico-Judaic textual and conceptual presuppositions? How, indeed, to justify such a critique, if not by magnifying and, perhaps even, 'glorifying' its innovative scope, both within and outside the context of religion? Once again, the deconstruction of Christianity, reduced to a mere surviving scripture (or writing), still more Greco-Jewish than Christian, more Christian than 'Christic', taken together amounts to a Christianity of survival, which seems to resonate with the present situation. The 'general textuality' of deconstruction resolves the problem by means of an infinite differing and deferring of faith-as-writing and the real-as-text, founding itself upon this reversibility that forms an asymmetrical content. But writing, along with its unilateral symbolic burden, can no longer be reduced to language, understood in the dominant linguistic manner that would give rise to deconstruction. The text of Christianity can be deconstructed, certainly, but not faith or the text-according-to-faith, determined by faith, beyond the level of signifying and signified, which is no longer the essential place of truth and still less the milieu of the True. The voice-in-person, the unique voice – that is, the in-voice, the radical voice, non-phonocentric – is the silence that determines in-the-last-*phone* scripture (or writing). Should we speak here about the Glorious Body of faith? Yes, of course: the Glorious Body of the voice that ceases to be a surviving voice. Does this exhaust speech? Why not? Should we go as far as posing the immanent *phonic Body* or a certain *phidelity*? Unless, of course, deconstruction cuts us off from speech, that is, the 'presence' of the Word? Let us here hail the 'Glorifiers of the Name' …

Glorious writing, risen among the signifying

Under what conditions do Scriptures – that is, sacred Scriptures in general – presuppose faith? But is not all writing considered, in some sense, 'sacred' in the context of a faith, since, without faith, they would be de-sacralised or produce the non-sacred? A call, request, an exhortation, or even efforts to reinforce faith are insufficient. Each expresses only external mechanisms, indicating mere affects and beliefs. Only their mode of being-manifested according to the being-given of their 'object' or cause is important. We have posed faith precisely as an *a priori* for donation and theologico-religious phenomenon. This form is not formal but material or lived and, therefore, is a real form or the Real of every form. There is nothing contradictory within this problematic. Yet whatever their interpretation may be, whether literal-fundamental, symbolic, hermeneutic, and so forth, they are, in general, supposed to be given, along with their sense, on the basis of a certain religious objectivation, like truths in themselves and for themselves. Philosophy is the inspiration, master, and beneficiary of such an interpretative basis. Sacred Scriptures and the Book are, in general, treated like correlates and supports for belief. They are not re-thought or re-worked according to the function of faith in such a way that belief becomes simply one of its *unilateral aspects*. Despite the appeals made to faith, in reality, such appeals call only to belief and its hermeneutic power, whereby religions suppose that sacred texts are more or less auto-comprehensible or auto-intelligible, certainly, and do not change the given in any essential way, being understood solely in terms of an auto-donation. By virtue of the distinction between faith in terms of an immanent Lived, that is, not 'interior' – a certain non-auto-sufficiency – and belief, unchaining and re-chaining religion again, any justification of scripture (or writing) in itself (the root of all fundamentalism), any efforts to ascribe to them an ultimate significance or final authority, is impossible. Indeed, doing so would reduce faith to a phenomenon of the subject's belief. Is there any need here to specify that this apparent devaluation of 'reformed' faith in scripture is not done for the benefit of a Church, guardian of dogma and 'truth'? The status of sacred texts – texts for propaganda, oppression, and simple ignorance – must be put back into question, so that we may see the decline of the excesses typical of contemporary understanding of writing and textuality, the banalization of the 'linguistic turn', which was already a properly Greek thought, and the cadaverization of 'deconstruction' – today an almost global *doxa* for intellectuals. Their destiny as Survivors is only beginning.

Theses, dogmas, symbols, and parables constitute, above all, the necessary meta-language for works and discourses that seemingly take for their object not at all a linguistic modality, proper to it, but rather an amphibology of theology and Man. Faith doubtless needs a meta-language in order to be posed and stated in axiomatic terms; it is no more mute and ineffable than it is exhausted in a discourse, but this must not be confused with language, which would serve here only to pose faith in the world. Faith needs structures or apparatuses in order to exist and produce works; it is no more a private affair or a matter of inner piety than a public display of pomp. Faith determines or transforms everything into non-religion, not the inverse, like religions, which, at best, only determine themselves reciprocally with it. Faith only consummates writing on the condition of gathering together and consuming its sufficiency. It forces a mutation in religious content, a messianic scripture or writing, without any announcement *in* the world, owing precisely to the fact it is an announcement *for* the world. Rather than attempting to decipher the hidden meaning of the Gospels with the nostalgic air of fundamentalism, either adding or subtracting distance upon distance, and refusing to acknowledge that this is now definitively lost and, more than lost, vanished or absent, wholly missing 'from' the texts, the faithful ought to produce the sense and meaning of the Scriptures in the very act of their transformation, according to the function of the *a priori* of faith. From the perspective of contemporary thought, man is a textual or linguistic animal – after having been rational – that is, a reading animal, who does not hesitate to incinerate and burn himself at the same time as his books in order to make his life into a living hell. But we-the-without-religion stopped believing in certain texts of philosophy, not only religion – that is, ceased to believe that the Real took refuge and now shelters at the very foundation of them.

What to do with these 'surviving writings' if not make a Glorious Writing? Contrary to the deconstruction of philosophy and theology, we appeal to a *risen or non-religious scripture.* As soon as man stands at the tomb, the tomb is empty of Man. What remains is the remnant or relic left behind and stripped bare, namely the subject, like the remnant of scripture that lies at the very foundation of the book. No more than Man, scripture according-to-faith is not 'inhumable' in either the signifying earth or the signified heaven. We admit that the symbols of faith, although articulated in words and through language, possess the same structure as faith. The nature of the symbol cannot possibly be understood starting from linguistic content and divisions; such devastating empiricism and positivism only interests intellectuals scarcely interested in philosophy, as can be seen, in the end, with the example of deconstruction. Recall that faith is unilateral, excluding whatever can be suspended from belief, and tolerates a supplementary and generic 'half-'belief – an original structure that is a 'half-'ecstasis, a relation-without-relation that brings the world but remains itself essentially only faith. The symbol is also understood as a unilateral duality. It is, therefore, an Identity that refuses any *a priori* linguistic distribution, however this may be done. The Identity of the symbol is the invisible and glorious 'side', that is, what the linguistic symbol becomes when given or manifested 'in-glory' or, put another way, resuming an old formula, when it is *risen among the signifying.*

A non-Catholic thesis for the use of the Reformation

How to identify the given or fact of scripture? How to interpret it? 'Scripture alone' is the rule of faith for Luther. But how can faith be a rule for faithful reading, if every rule is given by scripture? In order to leave this vicious circle, respect for scripture demands, precisely, the primacy of faith but also the reduction of the transcendent concurrence of scripture to the status of a symptom. How do such demands fit together or resolve this problem? This traverses the religious Reformation and the logical Reformation (of philosophy) in parallel. Each has already been accomplished. Scripture and Logic have in common the means for the reformation of religion or philosophy in accordance with the function of a new test or witness of truth. But they are only new writings that displace or shift the problem a little further along. A reformed logic of philosophy is insufficient in the same way the Reformation is for Protestantism: the single logic governing both cannot be the rule for their respective (auto-)interpretation. This would fall foul of the 'Catholic' objection made against the claim for scripture alone. The solution put forward to break the vicious circle gathers together the insufficiencies of Protestant Reform and analytic philosophy that suffuse and permeate the means for a reformed logic. Faith and logic do not seem to posses what they need, namely an immanent norm for truth. The 'Catholic' objection is admissible in the first instance insofar as scripture as well as logic needs an exterior attestation, or at the very least a critique of any claim to auto-foundation – a Papist or Roman Gödel showing that faith, like logic, cannot found itself. In reality, the Gödelian objection is itself limited in scope, not simply denied but rather admitted at the time as restricted in its universalization. In order for such a critique to be possible, writing itself must no longer be perceived from the outside – that is, philosophically or epistemologically, for example – and grasped in and by a system of auto-foundation; rather, it must be reduced and simplified, determined by an immanence at once radical and non-sufficient in a similar fashion to a generic faith that is no longer philosophical. Faith is not programmatic at all and the generic hardly more so. *Faith alone* ... can guarantee writing, but only a faith that transforms writing through a 'de-Catholicizing' process and making it thus truly universal, thereby transforming the works of the world into immanent works. The Man (of) faith is aimless insofar as it pursues only an immanent work. But this does not indicate an absence of work, rather, perhaps, a 'non-work'. Faith is foreclosed to work; it does not itself become a work but rather determines in-the-last-fidelity the writing of the work as a non-religious work.

This 'thesis' is, therefore, not anti-Catholic but non-Catholic, producing thereby a universality in another manner than the Roman one, determining in-the-last-instance Catholicism itself. It un-does the notion of 'Whole-Church' along with the duplicity and vicious authority that sustains it and is not content with its 'withering' or diminished state as survivor. Yet, in a certain way, this thesis is also non-reformed, even though it must comfort the Reformed in human solitude, if not the religious exclusivity of their faith. Faith, understood according to the above thesis, allows us to exit from the context of intra-Christian conflict. But we are not so naïve or even cunning as to claim that this conflict has been thus accomplished or, indeed, lacks any object. Is there an antinomy of salvation, works or faith? Such an antinomy seems, from a modern, contemporary perspective, too simplistic. But this antinomy (and others) is only set into the world in order to draw the terms together, rather than abolish them, so that they may survive. From this perspective, the celebrated and traditional arguments of Father François Veron (against the Reformation) can serve here as a guiding thread or symptom. It is possible to transform the questions posed by Veron to the Reformers and their absolutization of scripture into *non-Catholic theses*, that is, invert them in order to pose *an immanent but non-scriptural criterion of writing* that admits or demands at the same time, but not at all with the same qualitative force, transcendent decisions and choices, arising from a Church authority destined to furnish material for a dogmatic symptomatology, for the purpose of transforming them. Dogmas are, then, nothing other than a necessary conjectural material – a kind of first material, nothing more – for non-religious works. This is the materialist or material side to the thought of the last fidelity. In other words, scripture alone cannot furnish the ultimate rule(s) for interpretation. There must be criteria (or at least a criterion) that are not transcendent but, perhaps, goes sometimes as far as infallibility, as the Roman Church demands. Yet these criteria must be heteronomous, that is, radically immanent, too. Faith excludes opposed theses. This amounts to an immanent criterion *contra* any Church or worldly authority but remains itself non-sufficient or, at least, in need of a material for authoritarian decisions that it subsequently dualyses, undoing their authority. In the end, real infallibility can be found in faith, whence all is judged, but only on condition that there is something like a Whole to which faith does not 'suffice'.

1. What criteria does radical or 'generic' faith contain in order to select scripture? Such faith admits transcendent criteria for authority of any kind, even ecclesial ones, but they are inevitably only occasional and grant to scripture (or writing) only the pertinence or relevance of a contingent condition. Transcendent criteria cannot contribute to the determination of faith, which, although non-sufficient, remains the universal *a priori* that determines scripture

(or writing) in-the-last-instance, transforming the statements faith identifies and treats them as symptoms.

2. What grammar or 'dictionary' does this faith contain? An occasional or contingent grammar and lexicon that forms the 'language' in which it writes, with philosophy and theology, even Catholicism, serving as a meta-language. But this same grammar and dictionary that intervenes in the world of religion can only be received on condition that both are also treated as symptoms, transformed into unilateral structures, consumed in their normative sufficiency.

3. What logic or system, more generally, does this faith contain for the production of statements, starting from other statements? This more general 'logic' is precisely the consummation of any authority of the system or Church at the very heart of the unilateral consumption of such statements – that is, the logic of the duality that unifies-without-synthesis, in the immanence of faith (faith and religion), and unifies them under the non-religious form that emerges, *ex religione*.

The three foregoing arguments displace, in-verse or uni–verse, for the benefit of an alternative authority to mere writing, and so contain therein a 'reformed' or reforming use of Catholicism. But this *non-Catholic Thesis*, so to speak, is not simply a Reformation thesis, which remains incomplete and opposed, in a simplistic manner, to the practice of authority and servitude in Catholicism. On the contrary, the Reformation is assisted by this supplement or support, finding in the 'reformed', non-Catholic thesis a more direct source, namely Man, more interior than any interiority, but on the condition that the Man (of) faith is not confused with the believer. Once this support is attained, however, there remains the problem of determining a re-writing, which would be the agent of consummation, according to the faith of religions. Engaging in the struggle against fundamentalism and authoritarianism – the two major *vices* of monotheistic religions – the non-Catholic thesis will draw from them, in particular from Catholicism, the necessary material in order to reduce them to the state of a symptom, while practically denouncing, but not dogmatically, the theoretical weakness of a formal Protestantism, without content.

The reduction of the Roman Church and Reformed confession to the status of symptoms is not an indifferent act of levelling. Despite the insufficiencies of this simple scheme, generic and unilateral logic clearly presupposes the primacy-without-hierarchy of faith over any Church, and, therefore, in the sphere of models now, the determining primacy, again without hierarchy, of the Reformed confession over and above the Roman Church, which (pro)claims itself to be the unique paradigmatic image on earth of the body of Christ. But this does not indicate any hesitation that sometimes assumes a shifting, changing image, drifting into the sufficient essence of the Roman *catholicitas*, born from the combined force of St Paul and the Roman State. In the wake of both forces, various confessions, then sects, dreamt of constituting great and small churches. It is not certain that the body of Christ may be a Catholic one – a global or total Church – as St Paul and philosophy would like to persuade us. The body of Christ is the Body-One, that is, the Glorious Body of each and every member of the faithful. The Church, in contrast, remains a surviving and deathly body that has sur-vived, that is, sur-lived, the Pauline turning.

Fidelity as a rigorous method

Our problem is very much to transform and render faith to Man in terms of a practical decision, presupposed by works, but not to inculcate him into the famous 'disciplines', either through the active forcing of the churches upon the 'visible body of Christ' or through the work of the concept and the various operations accompanying it. What matters is the ousting of the All-Idea and the All-Church, that is, the world insofar as System – the Hegelianism that menaces all philosophy and theology. Such terms now acquire a different accent or more complex structure: as duplicity, an hallucinated mirror, or real-transcendental hallucination. This is the reason why we cannot resolve the problem through a simple reversal of Hegelianism, variously deployed and worked in contemporary thought (materialism, existence, or phenomenology, through the individual, understood as either 'sensible' (Feuerbach), 'religious' (Kierkegaard), or 'Living' (Henry). The individual no longer reverses philosophy in order to leap into the religious but rather *inverts and even renounces such an operation in order to assume the religious like a performed Inverse* of philosophy and theology. Man 'turns' philosophy and religion outside itself and, if someone must leap into faith, then this is for the philosopher and theologian to do, that is, to assume the decision of faith. But given that there is no leap into faith that is not already 'in-Man', science must leap outside such claims and pretensions in order to 'turn' into unilaterality.

Sola scriptura or *sola fides*? Faith alone is autonomous but non-sufficient. Work alone suffices even less. Considered in itself and for itself, scripture and work have no relation to faith and are, indeed, factors of belief and the imagination. They are not even aware of an hallucination. If faith had a principle, then it would be a non-sufficient Principle of Faith. But works are apparently and always sufficient. It is precisely this character of works that lays the pitiless trap, pushing those that work towards the Roman Church. The opposition between faith and works, along with their duality and their scholastic justificatory dialectic, is the worst articulation of the cross of theology – the special hell for theologians. Faith must, instead, *be treated by the rigorous method of the Cross insofar as determined by the Risen one*. Christ is the last of 'last things' – the ultimate witness of Human Glory – and the immanent proof of faith as well as the method for treating in-the-last-instance the problem of knowledge that so vexes the human multitude, even if the becoming-world of Christian confession, whether global or local, tends to efface or render imperceptible this kind of theological distinction by drowning them in the flux of History. We will take care not to imagine that all this has been 'overcome' or 'surpassed'. The struggle is never 'surpassed', never 'done', but can be 'set in place' – its secret authority inverted and limited to history or belief alone, making philosophical, not human, sense. This method is necessary for a mutation in theological conflicts: faith set against the Catholic transcendent norm of works, but also against all sectarian fundamentalism. Works are immanent insofar as a writing or faithful re-writing of dogmas.

Belief clearly organizes the traditional distribution and share of faith and works, albeit through an unstable line of demarcation, transcendent and ceaselessly re-traced, where theologies continually battle. The distribution of the Un-shareable is not a fact of faith, which is Un-shared, but rather the work of belief. Yet taking something for 'true' is already a work that is often confused with faith as Lived, which, in contrast to belief, does not leave ecstatically from itself. The only form of fidelity that is not already immediately twisted and bent out of shape is the faithfulness of the Man (of) faith. Fidelity and faith are indivisible, identical in-immanence, and constitute the complete concept of Man-in-Man, which alone brings to revelation the non-religious. This is the reason why there is fidelity in the Last-Instance, but, above all, fidelity is itself the Last-Instance. The faithful spirit is not preoccupied with harmoniously combining faith and works, producing thereby a good and fair distribution. Such a faith is condemned to be 'missioned' in works that the world calls forth. Will the mission of faith be thus understood no longer in terms of missionary proselytism, like, for example, St Paul?

A theorem of salvation as work

The theorem suits fidelity as well as logic. Given the real axioms of faith and the material imaginary of dogmas, in the broadest sense, such a theorem results from faithful writing, understood in terms of a rigour of-the-last-instance of immanent works. This assumes the status of non-religious theorems. The confession of faith is made by means of an axiomatic symbol in the form of a theorem that assures us – the 'performer' of faith – of salvation under certain conditions. This constitutes a work proper to such a confession. A decision must be made in order to tear faith out from the duplicity of the world that appropriates it. Such a decision is not done absolutely – that is, in a doctrine or mathematically in a positive axiom – but rather in an axiom that is the non(-act) human acting upon the world. Salvation is not a religious myth of Resurrection but the transformation by faith *from* here-below and *for* the here-below of the subject-world – that is, disalienation as the Glorious Body in-the-last-instance. There is no other non-imaginary and non-mythological content of salvation than under the practical form of theorems, transforming the material of dogma, concepts, and beliefs that articulate belief in the world itself. Yet this still concerns salvation understood as work, for there is no salvation specific to Man – the saviour as Glorious Body – but only the subject. This is not, then, a secondary activity for the preparation of salvation, confined to the earth, where we would await the realization of a promise. Faith is not faith 'in' or 'for' the Resurrection, like a belief in a mythologeme; it is no longer modelled on an event that subsequently organizes time around the idea of return and the disposition of hope, but rather the 'performed' coming of the Christ-subject. The confession of faith is an immanent work, with or without the Church. Better than a performative, such a confession is a performed-without-performance, determining, through its identity, the 'performation' of promises and their accomplishment.

Unlike the Man (of) faith, the subject is over-determined by various religious phenomena. The religious character of such phenomena gives them a theological or, more generally, objective form – as if faith and works of faith were adequately captured by appearances that grant them a sense, destination, and religious objectivity within the transcendent horizon of history and the world. Through this religious over-determination, the subject devotes itself. At the other end of the spectrum, faith transforms concrete onto-theo-logy – that is, existence – with the rigour of a theorem. We believe that faith does, indeed, raise mountains, but these are the mountains of religion and positive philosophies.

Faith does not, therefore, found but rather causes Identities to emerge, starting from given religious statements. This is accomplished through the 'weak force' of faith, that is, the positivity of its absence and being-separated. The axioms of faith are a way of unifying faith and the religious exteriority that expresses it under new forms, namely theorems. But this unification is no longer a superior synthesis realized by dogmas and the Church; rather, unification is a work in the form of a unilateral duality, bringing together an invisible side of faith along with a religious and theological appearance that is now simplified. By drawing its force from being without objects, from being the action proper to the non-action of Man, faith reveals the Strangeness of the non-religious to the world, not through an overcoming but through an immanent practice. It does not concern so much an effort to 'surpass' or 'raise up' mountains but to 'lift from below' and '*ex*-pose' them. In other words, salvation escapes history but not Man, who uses this history, not only for the purpose of formulating the axioms wherein faith is confessed but also to live a transcendental theorem of salvation.

Two forms of atheism: Conformism and heresy

Are 'we, the-without-religion', not still concerned with God and His armaments, and the structures of the Church? The twentieth century has confirmed the experience of some people, who felt abandoned by God, as Christ recognized Himself thus on the Cross. Whatever may be the historical truth of such experience, it must be set at the level of a universal experience of an immemorial affect, which, from the generic point of view, must be generalized for all people prepared to confirm it. But this must be restricted to people disabused of the indecent propaganda of the victors and preachers of any kind of obedience. This latter deception can be assumed universally in the way Christians do for original sin and Jews for the absence of God during the trial and rupture of the Covenant. We make, therefore, divine intervention into a *tabula rasa*. Such an intervention is a radical deception, without common measure, used sometimes by philosophers – for example, radical doubt, even the death of God or, further still, the end of philosophy – and bears witness to a weak atheism and the return of idols, preserving, in some form or another, the activity of philosophy as a final recourse. Radical atheism carries another meaning here: it does not measure the existence of God against His non-existence, like many philosophers argue, but His supposed goodness against real malice. On this point, the Jews are much more superior, measured against their misfortune and unhappiness, compared to the

Christians and their good sentiments. The former do not have the tepid and lukewarm idea of posing the problem of God on the terrain of Being, belief and non-belief, but rather the Other or the One. This latter opens the door upon heresy. What is worse, more incisive than a shameful atheism is an avowed *a priori* heresy, admitted and declared *before* any possible denouncements from conservative forces within religion, that would otherwise overwhelm any heresy, for occasional and conjectural reasons, without knowing what motivates them, causes their fear, their reactions, and their auto-defence: the fear and shame before Man, who has divined the wickedness of this God. Even atheists believe in a good God and practice forms of Church and religion. If there were, indeed, a God, then He would be in every way good for Man – this is the unconscious rationale of atheists, who believe, rebelling on the basis of a simple unbelief. For such atheists, belief deceived them in their hopes and beliefs. Along similar lines, belief that the problem can be resolved by simply ridding ourselves of the 'image of thought' (Deleuze) in order to obtain, in the end, a thought without representation will be avoided. Such theoreticism is cunning yet weak, supposing still the goodness of thought, albeit without image.

The posture assumed here is non-atheism, which is no more belief in *a good God* than a *belief* in a wicked God. The true heretic does not believe in a bad God, in the way someone believes in objects that have been badly manufactured, like a divine watchmaker might make bad watches. Belief is unilateral: the heretic has a belief that is *faithful* to the defectiveness of creation. Far from having lost faith, on the contrary, non-atheism is a fidelity to the disaster – more than a philosopher, who believes only in chaos. What is the criterion for the struggle against religion? Not atheism, but radical heresy. How can one be satisfied with an end of philosophy that is itself philosophical, either a moral death of God – founder and guarantor of the moral – or a negative image of Reason? Gnosis poses to religion much more profound suggestions, for example: (1) the world is bad due simply to the badness of the Creator, but a 'good God' cannot come to judge this world, only Man, who is not a subject; (2) Man must, then, assume primacy and judgement over God.

How the without-religion adopts religion

The Man (of) faith forms the basis for a critique of religious deception and the propaganda of priests. But Man is not thereby a 'Voltarian' so much as a 'Rousseauian' and a 'Marxist'. If the Man (of) faith abhors theodicies, taken as illusions cast upon human naïvety, then this is not on the basis of a belief in their empirical status, rather their transcendental character, which can be precisely transformed through dualysis. We are no longer bound to philosophy, understood as onto-theo-logy; we can break ourselves free from this covenant between philosophy, God, and Being. In short, we can *break the alliance between Western man and philosophy*, even if we retain and employ what remains. This old alliance is no longer a factor of truth and salvation, only a symptom to exorcize from the infernal vocation of religions (in historically and culturally diverse degrees) and a material to transform into a work of salvation. In reality, if one measures this problem against Judaism, then there has not been an alliance with philosophy, only an imaginary identification of Man with philosophy. The problem would thus come, instead, from a different kind of alliance, one that is sober, without illusions, and minus Jewish election. But can the Man (of) faith admit an alliance with an existing thought, like philosophy? The supplementary step, the last, in the sense of 'in-the-last-instance', consists in passing from the imaginary identification to an elective alliance, that is, from the latter to a unilateral alliance or covenant – in short, a non-religious adoption of philosophy. Opposite the 'conversion of the soul' that still reigns in philosophy, we oppose the adoption of thought. Over and above philosophical reversion – that is, the idea of a 'return' of thought into itself – we prefer uni-version, as a single act of the Man (of) faith.

In order to finish with the oft-repeated refrain of the 'end of philosophy', that is, birth and death, origin and posterity, in short any notion confusing philosophy with a life cycle of a natural species – an infantile and spontaneous theory made only about itself – we are condemned to adoptions. Philosophy no longer chooses or calls us, and Man is not the elect of philosophy or the animal elected by Reason; on the contrary, philosophy must be adopted and baptised, in order to be formed and transmitted for future posterity. There is a non-philosophical education of philosophers against the supposed spontaneity of their origin. Does this work of adoption still concern memory? This 'belongs' less to the past than a material or symptom from which the past is made; it calls for a transformative interpretation (i.e. unilateralizing), rather than a culture of memory. Given that Man and non-philosophy stand in a posture of primacy, the single law that can still be identified prescribes the transformation of the philosophico-religious form of the world and orders the unilateralization of God and the Trinity. Only intimidated and oppressed spirits can be frightened by this consequence and decry a naïve blasphemy. We not only claim God's creation but also respond to this in our own way, within the limits of human means, which is more than simply an abandonment of creation – it is the transformation of creation. Once the imaginary identification with philosophy and whatever remains of the alliance that made transcendence and a certain monotheistic notions operative are broken, we must reconstruct thought and its object, namely the old onto-theo-logy, which is no more than a symptom. Man has been the victim of theology and philosophy as well as the forms of the world and religion. In response, we invert this relation and assign to Man the determining function of primacy (of the Real), without simply reversing the situation or, even worse, taking vengeance against philosophy. What does Christ then come to do in this non-history? Christ is the first term for a non-Christian confession. Jesus follows the Law; St Paul reveals it. *Christ as the first term for a confession of faith* consummates or completes the break with the old religious covenant. Opposite God, as a mythological being, and Jesus, as an historico-legendary entity, Christ indicates the primacy of Man over the subject, that is, faith over belief. As for the historical Christ, He is the model of Man, introducing faith as the judge of belief. Once Man is no longer God or an image of God, there is a need for an empirico-historical model, which may serve as the basis for an interpretation.

Heresy as theo-fiction and philo-fiction

While a radical and generic theology may employ practical and rigorous procedures, reliance on the worst possible theological aberrations leaves open the greatest misunderstandings. 'Faith-in-Man' is, doubtless, a scandal, just as much as the notion of a theo-fiction. Such a faith is also an initiation test that could always be confused with 'faith in Man'. The Man (of) faith is a weakness, that is, a non-act that forces the subject to pass through the barrier of theology or traverse the circle of the duplicitous world called by a single name: 'Hell'. There is no other phenomenological hell than this one, which appears as the world in itself and for itself, starting from the saved world. The proper concept of heresy unfolds in the passage-in-force that traverses the dogmas of theology and the cavils and complaints of philosophy. Man is heresy-in-person and is thereby not divisible into causes, errances, and blasphemies, in order then to reunite them anew, but rather, being-separated, has already broken through this separation. If the transcendental 'sur-' mounts philosophical divisions by virtue of its unity, then heresy is what really traverses this being-separated in order to intervene in and upon the world. Man has been too often defined in a defensive and reactive manner in terms of resistance to supposed powers – this characterizes the entirety of philosophy over the course of the last century. In reality, Man traverses the resistance of the world as though traversing an hallucination. Heresy, as force (of) thought, occurs by means of clonage or mission rather than leaps; it is an Identity that passes as and by means of unilaterality. Heresy is not a 'traversal of immanence' (Deleuze). This implies one last interiority. Rather, heresy is a forced traversal of transcendence by immanence – the traversal of exteriority by faith.

Needless to say, contrary to proselytism, we do not ask anyone to 'believe' in the impossible affirmations posed or 'receive' such irreceivable theses. We do not, above all, claim simply that a practice of faith will lead to the rest 'logically' following from it. We do not even *believe* in a non-theological fiction; nothing about this is *credible*. On the contrary, we practice a theo-fiction. What does this concern, then, if not to free the Word from the Logos and grant this to Man, instead – this being who has not been created or programmed in order to speak or think solely – to be faithful to a logic and a faith, that is, to employ the language of the world and consummate or complete Hell? We are definitively free from the chains of language, which have been the instrument of our alienation, and not only in a philosophical manner. It matters very little that the most alienating – we call 'the Adversary' – may be religion or philosophy. We define ourselves as 'the without-religion' or as 'the without-philosophy'; hence, they lend their hands and distribute the division of work or labour. Religion is the most vindictive, the most beastly and deathly, force. Philosophy and theology are, broadly, set within the order of religion but furnish the conceptual, logical, and analytic framework most appropriate or adequate to articulate it. We must penetrate further and more deeply into the roots of every possible form of alienation, down as far as 'language' itself. This is clearly a far-too-simplistic formulation open to every kind of compromise and repentance. The most heretical formula does not absolutely exclude language through a self-contradictory gesture, like scepticism, for example; rather, such a formula declares: *the Real is foreclosed, like an Inverse, to language* (and to thought), and, further, the being-foreclosed of Man defines the status and possible usage of language. Such an un-chaining of Man barely amounts to an human enchaining of language but proceeds, in fact, from a double emancipation: a unilateral liberation of faith *and* language that Man transmits by the clonage of the Identity of the Real.

In order to gather together such effects into a formula, doubtless, too hastily, we call the emancipation of religious and theological language outside of itself '*theo-fiction*', and likewise with respect to philosophical language, we call '*philo-fiction*'. Both are determined by the employment of language by Man, the Emancipated-without-emancipation. The novel usage of the *old language*, namely the tongue of the '*old man*', is the messianic style, but a messianism where anticipation and expectation experiences 'in real time' (see above) the Arrival-in-Person. In virtue of its symbolic nature, determined in-the-last-instance by Man, the liberated Word also enjoys a human Identity, through this messianic force, lying at the very heart of the exteriority found in the theologico-philosophical world. This does not concern only the fusion of the theologico-philosophical and the spirit of science-fiction, their 'ultimate' or 'last' determination, but also, from this fusion, the emergence of an event that is wholly inassimilable to the religious *doxa* of the world. *Theo- and philo-fiction are ways of recognizing in language the status of the Stranger-in-person and the Glorious Body.* There is no 'new language' but rather a new use of the old language and the alienating alliance with Man. We do not reconstitute a supposed Adamic language but a Christic language, which is completely different. The three elements of this language can be summarized as follows: (1) the human usage of language is no longer anonymous – something longstanding in religions and philosophies that lost the name of Man from the very start – and condenses the ensemble of effects on the world that accompany the *real absence* of Man in the world; (2) this absence possesses the character of the Stranger, misunderstood or reduced in some way to a transcendent identity, and, in the end, lead back to the status of a mere derivative or an alterity of the self, and language, too, is a Stranger, carrying the same Identity as Man but associated this time to relations with the world (designations, significations, indications, reference); (3) this possesses a glorious or incorruptible nature. Theo- or philo-fiction are a way of obtaining an incorruptible or silent language, starting from the corruptible and noisy world. These are not, here, descriptions of a desirable state of affairs that must then be produced like a utopia in the imagination, but rather prescriptions or better still members of the messianic Word. The becoming-State of the Church and the becoming-Church of the State prematurely and almost by necessity suffocated heresy, which is the possibility *in-the-last-impossibility* that may still be offered to us. The final Ultimatum.

4

Dualysis of the trinity

Dualysis of revelation

Like any religious notion, Revelation has been pushed through the philosophical filter and undergone a tripartition. What is revealable – the foundation – must manifest itself to man, revealing either itself directly or through an operation of revelation (in Christ), which is revealed like a synthesis. This is sometimes the Revealing itself, at other times, the Revealed, which proves to be the Revealed *par excellence*. Theologians can be relied upon to refine, nuance, and displace this ternary and confect a Trinity out of it. But this hardly matters, what is essential for us here is to find another scheme for thought, more reduced than this tripartition, which, through an inversion, is philosophical only for Christian reasons. Man-in-Person is not a revealable thing, dissimulating potentialities and pretensions that nourish religious phantasms. The non-Christian will pose that Man is the Revealed-without-revelation, a veritable revealed to men, mixing itself with human substance. This revealed does not need an operation of revelation. On the contrary, revelation missions or clones the Christ-subject as revealing (or the operation of revelation). It reveals itself through struggle so that the world may appear, in the end, in truth, that is, precisely as revelation. Man is the Revealed-in-person, who renders impossible the revelation of the world. The world is not given like a revelation determined in-the-last-instance by the Revealed; rather, the world gives itself, first of all, as Hell, as auto-position or inherence in- and for-itself. The real or phenomenal node of Hell is only a sufficient auto-position to which the world is riveted to itself – but riveted twice, that is, in a duplicitous manner. The specific task of subjects is the transformation of the world. But this does not imply or involve the modification of forms or materials, like a transformed nature or society; rather, such a transformation involves tearing the world out from its auto-inherence in order to simplify it. This is not to be confused with a destructive philosophical gesture that tears up the old foundations in order to produce a new one. The effective work of the faithful subject consummates symptoms (or determined material) that shelter and protect the world-form, riveted to itself. The work of the faithful consumes the self-inherence or auto-reference that affects the world-form, but, in doing so, *reveals* the world-form – the unique objective of faithful work is the human revelation of the world insofar as adequate to Man-in-Person.

On the trinity as symptom

The Trinity is a symptomal form of the One-in-One or Humanity (uni-dentity/laterality/versality), set out and distributed through transcendence. The future non-religion does not make use of the One, properly speaking. This is contrary to mysticism and certain philosophies that do so in order to surpass and critique metaphysics (above all, the Multiple), relying always upon an initial distinction, for example, Being and being. The Christ-subject does not surpass or overcome the metaphysico-religious but, from the very start, turns towards the metaphysical and religious in a unilateral manner in order to explain and determine it. If philosophy plays out in Being and the Multiple, preserving for them, in the end, a kind of secondary status to the One, if the 'dominant mystic' attempts to place the One at the very centre of their scheme, without abandoning the ontological framework, then non-religion installs itself in-One, without any identification, in a way that no longer places itself at the centre of a philosophical circle but, instead, forms a relation to this circle in a relation-without-circle or, simply, in a unilateral way. The Christ-subject can thus make the religion-world appear as though possessed by an hallucination and a real-transcendental illusion that supposes the One has fallen, so to speak, into the sphere of Being and in some way can be substituted or exchanged with it.

The metaphysical decline of the One belongs solely to philosophy. There is nothing new here: all philosophy must announce the degradation and even decay of the One as a countable term. This necessary *decline* of the old One is even felt in the mystic-world, despite efforts to the contrary. Heidegger, for example, only reactivates the sense and concern for Being and the correlation with a *particular* being by trying to think this *outside* the reflection of being itself. This gesture combines the Aristotelian style of facticity, the more ideal style of Platonic surpassing or overcoming, and some notion of the *epekeina* (or beyond). Such a trio ends up covering almost the entire philosophical space and, in doing so, opens upon its very limit. Even if this does, indeed, open philosophy to the One (as limit), this does not resolve the problem of the specific 'trial' or 'test' of the One – this most recent ambition of thought that Heidegger, for example, like all philosophers, is content merely to brush against and glimpse, like a Promised Land, forever deferred. Before and after Heidegger there is a certain 'modern cut' made for the benefit of Being and the Multiple *against* the One. This scission inverts Heideggerian transcendence (towards the real One as Other) for the benefit of the immanence of the Multiple-without-One, thus displacing the demarcation between Being and the One (Badiou and Deleuze). Philosophers seem too busy filling the instance of Being with Time, the Idea, the Multiple, immanent Life or Affectivity, and so on. In doing so, they continue to reinforce the forgetting of the One up to the point where some even wish to kill it, like an old Greek god. It is like battling against a wind that ever turns the ontological wheel or like a watermill ever filling the casks of the Danaïdes.

The thesis claiming a 'substantial link (that is relational yet "real") within the Trinity' – like any theologico-philosophical decisions – serves only to overlay philosophical structures upon itself, rather than reject or really suspend them, thus making the faithful a believer or a shameful philosopher. When the subject is really detached from the God-world itself, then no ground or foundation can be any more made upon Man-in-Person, as if upon a God, an essence, or super-essence, since this involves always the same logic – the *beyond* man-animal or the *over*-man. Far from seeking within the subject's depths and 'nature' whatever might insert this term *a priori* into the transcendence and ends of onto-theo-logy, the humility and solitude of Man is content to exist *according* to its non-essence alone.

Only a resolutely human 'religion' can save the One from this symptomal decline, on condition of making humanity abandon the World and philosophy, and modify the concept and status of the human at the deepest level. The faithful subject ceases to decide, choose, desire, and so forth. But the Vision-in-One alone can abandon the will to renunciation, without casting a backward glance (Orpheus) – there is no 'underground-time' to the Arrived or Messianity. If traditional mystics still occupy the 'between-two' of heno-logical Difference, without making the least supplementary leap, then what we propose has, in contrast, crossed the ontological foreclosure of the One-in-Person and does so *according* to its very being-foreclosed.

The 'Trinity' is the ultimate object of theology, mystical or otherwise. We can treat it now like an absolute theological economy of religion. The Trinity is the ridge or precipice *par excellence*, where thought can topple from theology down into philosophy once again or be reduced to an *a priori* human, real, and, therefore, a transcendental content. If the super-transcendent Deity (Eckhart), more transcendent even than God, diffracts itself in a trinitarian manner, then the wholly immanent Humanity does not diffract itself in this way, but rather diffuses in a *a priori* manner into the three aspects that Man 'is', if the World is given: *uni–identity, uni–laterality, and uni–versality*. Of course, these aspects have their respective symptomal forms. Through their symptomal expression, they offer a real phenomenal content within the Trinity, but, importantly according to another organization and structure. *Uni–identity finds its symptom in the Father (destined to disappear in the Son), the uni–laterality of the subject finds its core or heart in the essence of the Son, and, finally, uni–versality finds its heart in the Holy Spirit.* Uni-laterality is the real and transcendental aspect that distinguishes the Christ-subject from the One-in-Person (and corresponds to the autonomy of the Son insofar as sent by the Father). Uni–versality – the Real as One – corresponds to the Holy Spirit, that is, the spirit or universality of God transmitted to the Son, and can be understood with respect to the subject insofar as *for* the World. In this way, the mediation of the One via the subject holds good for the World. There is, of course, no bi-univocal correspondence between the Trinity and unilateral duality. The trinitarian economy is a repetition of the structure of the philosophico-theological Decision, a variation on a transcendent invariant in many respects. The Determination-in-the-last-humanity is an immanent and dual scheme – not at all trinitarian, without economy, but able to explain the theological form given. Father, Son, and Holy Spirit are religious figurations, partly mythological, of an absolute philosophical structure, but only the schema of unilateral duality can make this tripartite ensemble (i.e. the Trinity) appear as a worldly symptom of Humanity. Far from any reduction and re-appropriation, for example, Feuerabachian, Christianity is no more than a symptom and material, not the essence of 'man' in general but rather Humanity as non-essence, which determines a subject in terms of Christ.

On the trinity as circumcession

The Trinity forms an homologous system with the structure of the absolute philosophical Decision. The instances (or persons) of the Trinity return in a circular manner, one to another, despite the famous 'distinction' of persons, that constitutes and animates, according to some theologians, a *circumincession*, whence they are and flow into one another. But this reciprocal return into one another does not exclude the possibility that one of them is distinguished from the others and may be a real transcendent term – positive or even, in negative terms, a withdrawn term – that supports the reality of the trinitarian ensemble. The circumincession of the Trinity, if thought a little more rigorously, without the restrictions and fetishes of theologians, must therefore be said as much to be a *circum-excession*. Mystics and theologians, above all in the Eastern Church, have tried to tip this structure over into a more immanent function and thereby modify the regime of the Trinity in order to withdraw it from the most speculative and absolute philosophy. The partially dehiscent circularity that tolerates this kind of philosophical structure *par excellence*, conjugating equally *meta-* and *epekeina*, unity and distinction, is evidently destined to be anchored in a real term and to grant this term a kind of consistency of a philosophical type, mixing reality and ideality. Measured against the hypothesis that the Real is radically autonomous and against the unilaterality of the last-identity of the faithful subject, the dialectical articulation of this circumcession between non-separable moments of unity and difference, including the negation of negation (Hegel), and their comprehension in terms of a 'negative sum' that is derived from the recovery of the three 'persons' of the Trinity, does not take a single step towards the Real. If the Trinity is a barely modified theological articulation of the philosophical Decision, if such a decisional structure simply repeats and duplicates itself in an apparently more concrete manner, then there is no real change of terrain, that is, no shift towards the real, with respect to the most formal philosophical triad.

The situation only really changes when the subject, who founds himself or herself upon faith, is no longer presupposed in terms of a circular incession or excession, but rather in terms of Man or the Ceded-without-cession that determines and clones it. Never conceded, ex-ceded, or in-ceded through a cause, the Christ-subject is a uni-cession. The One-in-One is, in some way, ceded to us, without any possible excess or in-cess that might otherwise re-form a circle of cession and gift. The Ceded is understood here in terms of the primacy or power of determination that we pose in the first ultimation, that is, the 'generator' of axioms.

Any distinction or differentiation is foreign to the One, we thus assure it. Yet it is still necessary to specify that this applies to any and every transcendent distinction and, therefore, a bilateral one, too, since radical immanence – non-unitional (of) self – 'contains' a unilaterality that is not simply interiorized division or distinction. The 'more' immanence is a simple Identity, the 'more' separated it becomes, from the start, without any operation, without world, and the 'more' this is done, then the 'more' separate the world in-immanence becomes from the world that is spontaneously auto-positional. We cannot say with respect to the One-in-Person that it is, for example, 'infinitely above number' (Eckhart), but, on the contrary, that is, through an intrinsic poverty, incommensurable with number – One as well as Multiple – since it is able to determine them negatively or via its own insufficiency. The One-in-Person is not like the Deity, since the latter would be interior *and* exterior, immanent *and* transcendent to the Trinity of Persons – the purest articulation of the philosophical Decision. The One-in-Person never has any term or relation, number or quality, *not in the way negative theology lacks them but rather due to a determining practice in-the-last-identity*. If the subject or the Word exists in a multitudinous state, then this multitude neither adds anything to the One nor disperses it. If the One is neither one nor many, then this is due uniquely to the fact that it is being in-One, rather than in number. If there is an arithmetic multiplicity of instances (i.e. the vision-in-One, the subject-existing-Christ, the world as Hell or radical evil), then this triplicity is only an appearance and a representation that cuts them up into pieces, dividing them into isolated 'natures' and *dialectically* reunited, rather than being articulated in-identity or through clonage and opposed directly to the triune or trinitarian logic. There is, in reality, only one duality (i.e. a theologico-religious duality between the One and the world) and a single 'being-missioned' by the One that starts from the world and the Christ-subject in a way that is no longer only a synthesis but also a unilateral duality. The future non-religion is free from arithmetic, being neither three nor two nor an ensemble (or set); it is a duality-without-quantity. This is the radical 'simplification' of the Trinity, forming its real node – neither Greek nor Jewish – that the faithful retrieve through the force of humility and 'poverty'.

The non-separability that circumcession signifies – above all when this becomes an intercession or even 'circonfession' (Derrida) – is a transcendent image of the most immanent Identity that defines itself precisely in terms of a being-separated-without-separation (from the World). Uni–identity and unilaterality seem to simulate, under immanent forms, the principle of continuity and alterity. However, without being simply an inversion, they are the last metaphysical principles that model the One, constrained to the conditions of the world. The way we employ heresy here always passes through a reduction of metaphysical principles to immanence. But they are only symptomal givens and models for interpretations that are peculiar to the conditions of the World. *Henosis* means that the unition of Three ceases to be the alpha and omega. Unition becomes the non-unitional (of) self, owing to the fact that it is now unition in-the-last-identity. The non-Christian duality is thus *contra* the theological Trinity. This is the Ockham's razor for future Christianity.

Clonage is the real content of transubstantiation. Man-in-Person invests, albeit inalienably, the thought-world, here and now, the historic Christ and metamorphosis into the Future Christ. This is at once a de-substantiation and a uni-substantiation: de-substantiation insofar as the old metaphysics of substance, *ousia* or hypostasis, no longer has any pertinence, except as material, and uni-substantiation insofar as the Real clones in a uni-originary way, by definition, a subject determined in-the-last-humanity – itself archi-originary, the Future Christ. The insoluble question regarding the metamorphosis and conversion of subjects finds a solution in the uni- and archi-humanity of Christ, which corresponds to the 'Persons-in-Person' of a future non-religion in such a way that they are from now on without transcendent support, but not, importantly, without material – Humanity being no longer such a support or substance.

Any metaphysical mythology of the persons of the Trinity is reduced now to the state of symptoms and transcendent model, the Messiah-subject 'traversing' the substances. The human non-religion begins with the faith that suspends *a priori* the perfections and metaphysical positivities; in doing so, it continues the dualysis of the Trinity – along with the Persons that comprise it – terminating in the end with the mystical consummation of the world.

In-the-last-paternity

Man-in-Person (the 'Father') limits in-the-last-paternity the 'All-Birth' by cloning the New-Born. The confusion of the natural-order with the order of the human Real concentrates itself within paternity as much as in birth and filiation, giving rise to the Trinity as a theology-form and symptom of unilateral duality. Some theologians use a biological metaphor, claiming that the 'Father signifies birth'. Psychoanalysis and a certain Judaism have symbolized and formalized paternity, but without breaking with this ancient order. This rupture is consummated, however, when the Father signifies Man-in-Person as well as the cause of the 'being-born-without-birth' – that is, the paternal refusal, not of any birth, but the 'All-Birth' and the forgetting of the being-born insofar as the subject and phenomena associated with birth are set in-Identity. Man is this Father by being-born and not beforehand, not by any eternity and vocation. Birth does not transform the Father but rather transforms its symbols and symptoms; it only enters into the domain of first names, for example, on the occasion of the Trinity. There is neither metaphor nor even a paternal epikein-aphor, except in the symbolic order that maintains a partial link, in a constitutive manner, with the religious world. Such a Father, the Non-Sufficient-Father, who determines-in-the-last-paternity the

Son, is not, therefore, the Law, but can always, as a symbolized and formalized first name, designate the human cause.

A preliminary question concerning terminology imposes itself upon us now. This question concerns the designations of 'Father' and 'Son' with respect to the Real that no longer corresponds to any natural or social privilege, even symbolic, in the sense of the unconscious. Such a privilege is here more than simply transformed into a metaphor – it is dualyzed. We are, furthermore, condemned by philosophy, mysticism, and psychoanalysis, reunited once again like inevitable symptoms, even pathologies, to require such a term (like 'Sons' rather than 'Daughters') in order to designate Man-in-Man in an occasional relation to birth. The World obliges us to seek in paternity a designation for the human Real, insofar as the terms 'Man' and 'Son' have no determining or real sexual sense – in particular 'Man' but 'Son' no less so – but only an objective connotation that is apparent in sexual difference (i.e. with respect to the mother, where there is nothing to say except that this is not exactly the same thing as sexual difference but rather approximates an occasion). Man-in-Person and Woman-in-Person are not, in any case, the 'father' of Man, like the biologico-philosophical circle, only the father of Son- and Daughter-subjects.

With respect to the notion of the Father that does not suffice by itself at the birth of the Christ-subject, but, instead, through a 'negative' function, finds itself set at the end of auto-generation, like a fundamental phantasm, birth is only a necessary given within its own order in terms of a simple given that must be set in-Person for our conception of the Father. As for the New-Born as such, it has ceased to desire the Father or wish to be-the-Father, even, like some ancient mystics, yearn to reunite with Him in all-paternity. The Father is more than simply absent or missing, such terms are no longer appropriate, risking always being taken up once again into the general economy of the world. The Father is a necessary and non-sufficient condition, that is, 'negative' in this sense, for the Son. There is all the more reason, then, to multiply the number of persons and seek a Third Father – a Simple and Alone Father, with numerous designations. But we shall avoid doing this *ad infinitum*, like the Neo-Platonists and certain analysts. The Father is univocal insofar as cause and equivocal insofar as name or designated. There is no first name for the Father that is absolutely equivalent or carrying a truth value (true or false) beyond what furnishes the contingency of language. This forms part of the economy of thought-language, not non-theological knowledge. Even the unknowability of the Father does not signify that He may be unthinkable, since the first term 'father' is inserted amongst the axioms and suffices to think, without knowing, and thus makes knowledge possible. Such designations are, on the one hand, therefore, imposed by philosophy and other similar disciplines, revealing their own criteria of truth, but, on the other hand, they are set *in-the-last-paternity* by the Real and reduced to their form of first names. The heretical subject – that is, the Future Christ – stands alone against the worldly or authoritarian Father, revindicating birth as determining Man. But the heretical subject does so in the 'forced name' of the Unknown Father and, through defining and constituting it, frees the Father from the servitude of the name by confirming the identity of it.

The nature of the Father is not, therefore, simply to produce the Son by some mode of production but rather, through cloning, give itself to the Son, without reserve or alienation. He alone can cause the Stranger or Messiah to emerge for the world. The Son is the unilateral 'image' of the Father, without being in any way a part of the latter. If the Son has a role – that is, the subject in general – then this would be the vehicle and existence for the Father, adjacent to the World. This is an heretical and strange existence, representing nothing that already exists. What this presents, for the first time, is a world already transformed or saved. The Father and the Son are but a single man, that is, a lived, without sexual division – in the sense whereby they are identical in-the-last-paternity. The Son is an effectuation of the Father *through* (and *against*) the world, not at all His realization or actualization. Unlike the Father, the Son *exists*, and can be less easily denied or forgotten. The Father is separated or foreclosed to the Son and cannot claim to exist like the Son, but nevertheless knows that He is not alienated in the Messiah. The world hallucinates the Father and deludes itself with respect to the Son. This is the real content of the Trinity into which mystics and theologians continually try to import historical and religious figures.

How God becomes Son of Man

God must Himself become Christ-subject or the Son of man, starting from what He is – God-the-World, God-Hell.

Who is the historical and theological figure called 'Christ'? A symptom and a model, an occasion and restricted interpretation of the universal Son of man. The future mystic rests entirely upon a non-Christian practice of Christ and God. Clonage applies as much to theological things and God like any other thing. The creation of a new application of Christ lies within the capacities of clonage. It is through clonage that Christ can be treated, first of all, as a simple symptomal indication, then as a particular interpretation of the mystical subject, not as the sacrificed son of God – at once jealous and generous with His transcendence – but as a cloned Son of Man and, as such, a messiah for the World.

On this basis, *who*, exactly, is 'God'? The mystic who errs into an indefinite transcendence offers secrets from God, sounds out the depths and exposes Him, manifesting God, not phenomenologically but affectively, through love and faith – a response to creation. But the Vision-in-One, unlearned and given outside any revelation, can clone the Christian God. The thesis of a *theo-genesis* – that is, a becoming-God or the birth of God in the soul – can receive a non-worldly content if it passes over to the state of symptom. God is doubtless born, not as God but born-without-birth. God is not born in the soul dialectically but rather as being-cloned, starting from old, ancient forms. Under this state (of being-cloned), God is turned unilaterally towards the World and the ancient God-Hell. By becoming Son of Man, the new God can save the Old God. If *theosis* is a transcendent gift, supposed more or less explicitly in terms of a given instance or, at the very least, a transcendent donation, then clonage is something other than a becoming-man of God – it is wholly the inverse (note reverse): a becoming-God of man. God must emerge as Son, no more and no less than man, in order to give rise to and create a system with the World. Heretical radicality, which explains the symptom of historical and worldly heresies, places the subject in-Identity. This subject has the sole right to declare itself *neither God nor World*. But it is not exhausted in such statements nor reduced, in some fashion, to anarchism. The mystical subject neither seeks nor desires God *insofar as* God – therefore as Deity – but rather insofar as the *transcendental identity (of) God*. The mystic does not desire but *invents* God, inducing and deducing this from the Infernal God in accordance with the Vision-in-One. Reduced to the function of subject, Humanity invents the mystical God, that is, a God who dares renounce His own creation and withdraws from the World as Son, which is, first of all, given *for* the World.

5

A clandestine non-religion

The Name-of-Man

Theology mixes together the most ancient religious beliefs, historically uncertain events and fables, and, in the end, a philosophical framework that is problematic by definition, and then seeks to rationalize them. The purpose of our book is not to 'un-mix' this hotchpotch. Each of these three ways, above all the last two, namely historical research and philosophical invention, introduce variations that provide the ground or basis for the theoretical life of God but condemn theology to mere 'theoreticism'. Without discussing the mythological grounds for more barbaric representations and dispositions that change only very slowly over the course of a leaden and insistent repetition, the essential variation(s) can be found in the field of monotheist philosophy and ontology of God, where the worldly presuppositions drawn from Greek paganism have remained un-elucidated. Does this concern, then, an Heideggerian enterprise of repetition (*Wiederholung*), that is, a deconstruction of Christianity performed according to a demythologization, even an analysis of theological or ordinary language of faith? This would still be a work of philosophical therapy. Yet precisely with regard to theology, the transcendental illusion *par excellence* will have been to turn God into the adventures of onto-theo-logical Difference, that is, to believe that to philosophize could suffice and concerns research into the presuppositions that underpin its positive concept, namely, classical perfections, and somehow bring them to light in, for example, phenomenology. Such a project arises and unfolds within a broader critique that starts with demythologization, then deconstruction, which is a 'false step' – hesitant and staggering – marking simply the renewal of the same, most fundamental errors of the theology with respect to 'Being' and the perfections of God. It is always the same philosophical sufficiency, claiming secretly to comfort God and grant Him consistency. But this leaves open the admission that God may be extremely weak in the face of historical events, something that the philosopher identifies and seeks to correct. Even the persecuted Jewish people project the fragility of their existence upon God. After the triumph of God in the full majesty of Being comes the 'hostage God' of Abraham and Jacob; after the Great Watchmaker, the deconstruction of divine Watchmaking. So, what to do with the God of faith? This concerns the way in which God, by nature, is rarely, if ever, the God of faith, but the one of belief. This is a problem, since this does not concern beliefs at all. If God were so weak, so apt to receive the *a priori* designation of victim, then the completion of what the Jews began, namely, the stripping away of any name from God, becomes necessary. More than simply not pronounce His name, thereby keeping it reserved in an absolute memory, we *refuse* even this name to Him, not through an absolute refusal, which would still amount to 'not pronouncing' – hence, a deconstruction – but through a suspension that empties out from God any substance and 'irrealizing' it as a pure fiction of the Word, as onto-theology-fiction or as 'divine name' deprived of any referent. This would complete and consummate the namelessness of the Jewish God. 'God is God, name of God!', there has not been a more pagan formula, that is, religious and mythological, more Jewish, that is, anti-Jewish, more sensible, that is, tautological and devoid of sense. Being and the name presuppose one another; they are convertible and bear witness to the primacy of the Word. But this is too large a formula and even too sufficient. This is God 'thundering in the pulpit' like a classical theologian. Opposed to this thunderous God stands 'God without Being' (Marion), bearing witness to a humble thought, already faithful and modest. But God – that is, the philosopher, if not the theologian – still keeps watch over this becoming that always announces the law and its effects. The most decidedly 'religious' spirits remain pagan. They adore too much the name of God and fail to be sufficiently 'glorifiers' – they cannot attain a non-theological fidelity.

The problem doubtless concerns finding a way to name that is not ontological – that is, does not repeat the Parmenidian equation of language and being – but also to continue naming, even employing divine names. In order to avoid an ontology as well as ethics of God, along with the Greco-Judaic antinomy (Heidegger and Levinas), the name(s) of God must be treated as a symptom, something like a lapsus – a slip of the tongue – for another name, namely human, since this now concerns the Name-of-Man. This is our own way of being 'otherwise than onto-theo-Jews', 'otherwise than Greco-Jewish theologians', in order to give a way of unifying the Greek and the Jew in a radical manner – that is, a way that does not find support in historical givens or a divergent ethos but rather in the form of what we will call two 'religious postures' founded and articulated in fidelity. We will no longer pronounce the name of God, not in order to retain this name in our own way, like the Jews, but rather to hear another name there, from within an extreme banality or ordinariness, and be able to use this name, without fearing the wrath of the 'onomoclasts'.

Philosophical and religious paradigms

What kind of overcoming is neither the Other nor a return into the fold of Being? After Being or Paganism, Deconstruction or Judaism, immanent Messianity is the consummation of the theologico-religious; it is a new paradigm that has very little to do with the 'end'. This consummation is not a Greek 'achievement' or 'accomplishment'. It is the Last Thing or the Last Event arriving into the world. The Coming is identical to the consummation of the world or a philosophical mediation. There is no longer any mediation between opposed terms, like the old Hegeliano-religious, philosophical and Greek, schema might like to still practice. Christ is the immediate mediation, the consummation of pagan relations. He is the Mid-Place or even the generic. The *a priori* and then the subject fulfil the function of the organon or the 'means', but only in the Marxist sense, not the Hegelian one. This makes possible a radical comprehension of Christ that annihilates God *insofar as* a pagan residue, that is, the concentration of the pagan divine into a single God, pushing Judaism to the furthest, most extreme point of paganism (see above). The Judaic reduction of the world through an excessive transcendence is not yet the consummation of the theologico-religious. Christ renders God a useless God, whether one or multiple, as well as any sense of transcendence. He is the model for the 'last instance' not insofar as transcendence but according to the scheme of the Last Instance as immanence and the Other as unilateral duality. The work of Christ, assuming the Father or God by drawing them into immanence, is the consummation of religion(s), that is, religion understood as transcendence, worldly, and mundane. God has been made in the image of Man but precisely an inverted and specular image – an image projected upon the screen of the world. Christ marks a radical 'making immanent' of the Father in the Son, and the Son of Man means nothing other than this disappearance via immanence of God in Man and Father in Son. Christ causes transcendence to disappear from such paradigms but does not cause religion itself to disappear. Christianity remains a religion, but an immanent one this time, that is, a mixed form. Just as there are 'philosophies of immanence', there are also 'theologies of immanence' that do not completely reduce their theological and religious aspect.

There are three religious paradigms for philosophy, which is an autonomous thought, not a remainder of these paradigms. The paradigms are as follows: the Greek Cosmos, the unique God, and Christ. The philosophical dimension is a trinitarian structure that is not particularly religious. When religion is made trinitarian, then it is under the direct influence of philosophy. But the philosophical principle at work here, from a syntactical point of view at least, is a triangulation that superposes itself or overdetermines a religious paradigm, supposed to be paradigmatic of the Real. The philosophical is dominated by the religious paradigm of the Cosmos or cosmo-theological. Such paganism does not exhaust the philosophical gesture but rather transforms and modulates it. We could distinguish, in a very brief manner, cosmo-paganism, mono-Judaism, Christo-messianism (such doublets are evidently partial neoplasms). They correspond, respectively, to the primacy of Being, logo-centrism or metaphysics, the primacy of the Other as real or deconstruction, the primacy of the One as real or non-philosophical immanence. Non-philosophy treats not only philosophy in the strict sense of triangularity but also religious paradigms as material.

The two initial prejudices of all theology

The philosophical aspect to theology manifests the same prejudices that can be found in any other philosophical system or doctrine. If philosophers are fundamentalist theologians, then theologians are mystical philosophers. They share the same set of prejudices and illusions, linked to their spontaneous practice of thought. Such prejudices can take the form of a restricted distinction or separation with respect to a problematic that clams a field or identity called 'the' philosophy, on the one hand, and a sufficiency of philosophy and God that exhausts the Real, on the other. Both prejudices evidently form the basis for a system. The first cuts into the world, slicing into the objects and semantics, the organization and syntax, that constitute this world and poses them in terms of a Whole or Global philosophy that is supposed to elucidate the entire extension and complexity of it. The second decides that the Whole constitutes at least a shelter for God and man. On the one hand, the Whole is posed like a restriction or limit – an empirico-transcendental field – on the other, the Whole posed like an authority or real, constituting thought. In order to be philosophically universal, the prejudices that characterize the nature and function of philosophy are nonetheless fatal deficiencies that burden the theological enterprise after the philosophical one.

With respect to the nature of the Whole, indeed, this consists precisely in a triangulation (i.e. the transcendental Two and One form the most elementary constituents) that is very complex. It is a double triangulation, on one hand, empirico-transcendental, on the other, transcendental-aprioric. This double figure results from the *a priori* deduction of the Two from the transcendental One, making this Two itself transcendental, not empirical. Both triangles have a common term: the transcendental One. They form, therefore, a synthesis that is only a fivefold (i.e. with five terms, not six). But the

One is always by right, if not, indeed, historically, surpassed by a One – other and the same – that is this time the *transcendent* One, no longer transcendental. The philosophical, properly understood, is transcendental, but the structure of the philosophical architecture, when fully developed and deployed, contains a 5/6 arrangement of terms. This architecture finds itself crowned by a religious paradigm or a primacy that is supposed to amount to the Real. On this basis, philosophy believes itself to be the absolute Real (Hegel and Nietzsche, for example), needing, in some sense or other, a theological limit-experience in the same way it needs an opposed empirical base or scientific order. We will call this superior dimension that crowns the transcendental Whole 'the Real' that is, in essence, religious – at once *beyond* philosophy and touching or even mixing itself there. This dimension functions very much according to doctrines like the One, the Good, or even the Beyond, like the Other or divine Life. This Whole is restricted by doctrinal as well as specific systematic divisions. Idealism and even Materialism pose the Whole under a still restricted form, but for other reasons. They pose the primacy of the Real but do so under a divided form, as if there were two Reals or two primacies. What this proves is that the Real remains secretly posed in a restricted manner, as divided or transcendental. This explains, in part, why the theological divisions and splits, performed through the classical ontology of perfection, anthropology of creation, divine transcendence, and so forth, do not register, from the very start, the complexity of philosophical synthesis in terms of the fivefold (5/6), and, instead, spontaneously trim and cut it. They all form some kind of vicious circle, feeding from the great circle of mythology and beliefs. But the philosophical impulse clearly continues to suffuse and innervate such restricted divisions. With respect to the possible function or the Real of this philosophical synthesis, traditionally assumed by God, it is evident that the principle of the primacy of Man, foreclosed to the Name of God (and even in a sense to the Name-of-Man), implies a suspension of the pertinence of the Whole, and, therefore, the uprooting of any philosophical and theological Whole by the *a priori* of faith. The indivisible Real or One can only be desire, since this is linked to the divisible or transcendental One, brought up through this to its peak. If the real One were truly the Real-in-Person, then it would be separated, whereas, here, it is not independent. The One is never given as separated but always included in a religious whole or totality of beliefs and transcendence(s) – it remains a mirage of philosophical or common beliefs. The transcendental Whole is a simple duplicity and torsion. If one adds the in-divided One to this transcendental Whole, then this addition does not remain exterior, religion and Logos remain associated and united, co-penetrating one another. This is the theo-logical Difference that is not dissimilar to scientific or philosophical difference; rather, it is a kind of superior duality – a real-transcendental, not an empirico-transcendental duality. The empirico-transcendental is the dominating Two and the dominated One; the real-transcendental duality is the dominating One and the dominated Two of the divisible One. There are, then, first of all, the extreme terms of the Transcendental and the Empirical, then the intermediary terms or the organon of the *a priori*. But the real indivisible One is needed in order to re-link a second time the ensemble into a Whole that finishes in theology and the desire for the real One or the Idea. But the Idea is desire – it is the philosophical desire. Philosophy is the middle, 'hard-working' zone for thought, but not the base or foundation of religion. Whereas science is the 'hard-working' zone for philosophy itself, it is like a religion for the sciences. The two levels of duplicity must be suspended: the first level – the superior or religious – suspended by the Real and the second – the properly philosophical – by the subject. Does this mark the index, perhaps? Does this indicate the symptom of radical immanence that is theologically impossible or reputedly pantheist? Religion and philosophy, which have come together and have been linked in a different way to the relationship between the science and philosophy, cannot, indeed, be separated.

Philosophy is then, when fully developed and deployed, a quintuplicity (or fivefold), that is, a double triangular duplicity that at once makes the *meta-* and *epekeina*-physical duality of onto-theo-logy concrete and accomplishes the necessary link in the One, supposed real and the model of God. The 'fivefold' synthesis does not, however, hold for the three monotheism (above); it is the single, unique structure of the real One – the onto-theo-monism that holds for all philosophies, even the Greeks. Neither Judaism nor Christianity, which are no more or less rejections of the world and philosophy, can push the analysis of the world as far as, and employ the same philosophical potential, as the Greeks. But they are the rigid, enduring, and exclusive forms of monotheism that permit the deployment of the richest and most structured content of thought. The condition for non-theology, which analyses theology with the least risk of forgetting the One, can be found in grasping the structural affinity of the Greek One and the God of religions *inversely*, that is, not to reject the world as vanity and folly, like an object of hate or confusion, but understand this architecture in its entirety, with the 5/6 dimensions of the fully developed and deployed Whole, resting at once upon the Greek Cosmos and Religious Monotheist model. The religion-world is the real adversary, perhaps, forming a new duality like the one between science and philosophy. Is religion the real, monotheist coronation of philosophy as structure, forming a special duality? What term plays the dominating and which the dominated? It is possible to imagine three ascending orders: science at the base, acting as determinant, transcendental philosophy or the transcendental 'whole' second, serving as medium or means – that is, an intermediary order or organon (see above) – and, finally, religion as the immanent coronation of philosophy.

The fully developed and deployed philosophy, adequately measured against its own identity, is a global 'over-' or 'super-functioning' machine that combines at once an under-determination and over-determination concerned solely with the production of surplus value through which only one part is either consummated, as the means of subsistence by itself, or 'lost' at each moment. The problem concerns knowing whether the surplus value is stronger than the 'sub-value' or whether the machine is equal to itself and thus able to compensate itself. Yes, philosophy produces a surplus value of systems, doctrines, and traditions and enriches or accumulates philosophical capital for the benefit and profit of all philosophers, with theological capital benefiting from the dividends. Philosophy always accompanies an Identity, indicating its ideal or imaginary achievement – that is, the Ideal of the self (or itself). We have, indeed, distinguished between the ideal Self, the transcendental One of philosophy, and the Ideal of the self or the real and superior One, which is theological *par excellence*.

A theory of radical evil

Is evil absolute or radical? In the philosophical context, absolute evil encounters some serious difficulties: 'evil' is a transcendental term lacking any absolute, effective content. The amphibological style of philosophy necessitates the combination of an empirical evil with an ideal or, in a sense, religious one. Such a combination is difficult to raise to the status of an absolute: is it exemplified – that is, in a singular yet absolute instance – in anti-Semitic persecution, the Shoah, for example? Terms such as barbarism, totalitarianism, and persecution barely seem able to exhaust the Absolute (in the philosophical sense) beyond their ethical appeal. An empirico-transcendental construction of an evil 'Whole' or 'Totality' is already problematic. Such a doublet imposes only modest and reasonable solutions that resolve themselves into ways of retreating before the contradiction found between the philosophical 'Whole' and evil. This presents itself, on the one hand, as the systematically deceptive, yet theoretically hypothetical and immediately masterable Cartesian Malign Demon that can also substitute for the real or indivisible One that crowns philosophy, and, on the other, as a Kantian rational concept of evil that emerges from a classical philosophical operation, resting, in the end, upon the reciprocal conversion between Good and Evil. Within both distinct philosophical forms, the two solutions to the question of evil remain interior to the inferior duplicity of the philosophical Whole. They are, however, for us at least, materials or symptoms. The question of evil declines in another manner when conceived in terms of a real-transcendental or superior Whole. A real Whole – ultimately the 'one' of evil – *'the' Evil* par excellence, that is, *indivisible or real that is the true sense of 'absolute'* is a contradiction in terms and unsustainable in the philosophical theo-logo-dicy. Another solution is therefore needed in order to apperceive this ultimate and supposed real Evil, something that is impossible for philosophy. This is very effective, but under a completely different set of condition for revelation: it is precisely a supposed or philosophically desirable Good that proves, in the end, to be Evil. In other words, the real or ultimate God that theo-logo-dicy employs in order to bewitch subjects, calling to them and chaining them to philosophy, is found to be *itself* Evil for the subject *human-in-person*. Put simply, the absolute Good is revealed to be 'radical' Evil in a new, non-Kantian sense, not as absolute Evil – in the context of non-theology, the Absolute is precisely revealed as being Evil – but rather revealed under the conditions of radicality.

We have not, therefore, simply reversed the hierarchy of Good and Evil but rather distributed the terms in another way through the introduction of a new causality, namely Man-in-Person as faith, that *a priori* reveals or gives the world (complete as having the form of onto-theo-logy and higher still of theo-logo-dicy) precisely as radical Evil, under the double form of an hallucination (real) and an illusion (transcendental), which together make possible and govern the crime. Faith is the *a priori* that justifies the equation World = radical Evil.

With many nuances made with respect to the particularity of the experience, thought, and re-vindication of the Jews, there emerges the possible inclusion of the Jewish God, as a wicked and insane creator, in radical Evil. This is done in accordance with a certain gnosticism that has been torn from its own religious particularity. Man-in-Person emits the faith that presupposes the world in a unilateral manner, making any failed or illusory creation impossible. A God understood and claimed to be the creator of the world or the source from which this world emanates or is deduced by filiation is a deceitful and, in any case, hallucinated God. From this can be drawn conclusions, for and against, Levinas, for example, as a major figure of contemporary Judaism: the idea of a 'first ethics' based on the epiphany of the 'Face' is an illusory conception of the Other, that is, a transcendental illusion (in our sense) of a religious-transcendent messianism. The Other is a wicked and persecuting figure, not with respect to man, as Levinas understands him, but the subject deduced from Man-in-Person, that is, from immanent humanity. The Other persecutes the subject insofar as deduced from Man-in-Person. What Levinas calls the 'goodness' of the Other, Man-in-Person reveals *a priori* to be a persecuting malice. Levinas transposed the experience and suffering of the Shoah directly into the site of philosophy but without, importantly, radically suspending it; rather, the conception of the Other reinforces the natural jealousy of the Jewish God with the hallucination proper to the Logos. We do not claim that the transcendent God is absolute evil, but rather that the absolute God is a radical Evil that seizes authority over and against Man.

Post-ecclesial faith as last belief

Once faith has entered into and been enclosed in the iron-cast circle of theology, having explored every philosophical possibility, what remains is still a belief that wants to leave this circle, asking how to cut itself from such institutional forms, felt, once again, as the most subjugating. This is the first and simplest reaction: dreaming of freedom. But it is precisely an ecclesial or Church-based faith that poses this problem, in particular, faith in the sufficient God of the classical perfections that the Church officially maintains. This is the great contemporary post-ecclesial aspiration, echoing the various deformations and innumerable sectarian deviations.

Why does faith wish to leave theological beliefs, even via a leap? This leap is symmetrical to the one needed in order to enter into theology in the first place – that is, from the initial *a priori* leap of faith into the Whole of the belief in itself and for itself. Having entered into religion, then into theology, both through the assumption of a leap, faith now wants to leave them in the same way via *another* leap and often cannot imagine anything else. From this perspective, there is nothing to believe or hope for except precisely a demythologization or a form of deconstruction of the ecclesial and theological institutions, that is, the eclessio-logical Difference. There is the closed door of the Greek Cosmos and the half-open, half-entered doorway of Judaic alterity that characterizes much in contemporary thought. The exit from the ecclesial remains very much conceived in a philosophical manner, that is, in terms of transcendence or a supplement of transcendence, which will set this in an authentic relation with the true God. But this is not all that the faithful subject can do, if he or she wishes to make one's exit. There is the *half-leap* (the *Mid-leap*). This is an hitherto unheard of opening of immanence that unfolds precisely as faith. What remains, then, is the transfer of Judaism on to this terrain of radical immanence. This involves the refusal of mediation as auto-mediation, substituting, instead, the primacy of the Real. Christ made this leap possible by reducing, through His mediation, the distance to be crossed. But this mediation must itself be made immanent. The distance typical of belief, giving only an appearance of faith, must be overcome, now being-replaced in Man-in-Person. There would no longer be any leap into faith in this sense, as into the Absolute, like Kierkegaard, only the identity in immanence of a *Mid-leap* that does not leap by and into the middle but displaces and sets itself within this middle. Man-in-Person does not leap into faith but rather is the pure messianity that unfolds as an *a priori* of faith. From the perspective of the world, there is thus only a half-leap from all possible theology as well as any form of the world. The needed half-leap is our responsibility as a subject, not Man properly speaking; it is determined *in-the-last-humanity as the Coming that is the real form of grace*. This half-leap of the subject in Man is not *countered* (Levinas) by an infinite God but *determined inversely in terms of a Coming or grace*. The subject must leap into the reality of Man, who is not the subject, that is, into the radical immanence of the subject that comes inversely or *a priori* before belief.

The end of beliefs and the exit from the post-ecclesial

Let us take up once again the philosophical roots of the problem of the 'exit' from faith, outside belief. We have shown *a propos* of

German Idealism that this problem, the great and single problem of modern philosophy, concerns a 'passage' outside of philosophy into non-philosophy. There is a symmetrical problem, albeit theoretically less apparent, with respect to the passage out of theology that we will call, in a still undetermined manner, a non-theology. This problem, put in more concrete terms, concerns the exit from the authority of the Church towards a more authentic and more ecumenical faith. Let us suppose that there are three philosophical ages: the One as multiple or Being (including the Platonic hypothesis of the *Parmeniedes*), the One as Other, and, finally, the One as One or One-in-One. They are accompanied by parallel epochs: the age of the gods, the unique God, and, finally, Man-in-Person. This is an extremely simplistic and schematic logic, independent of historical circumstances, but nevertheless suffices for our present purposes. Contemporary thought continues to perpetuate, via new means and methods, the relation between Being and its own self-surpassing as Other in the philosophy of language, Judaism, and psychoanalysis. But such disciplinary supports are contingent; philosophy follows a logic that is not especially linguistic in nature but rather conceptual. We have been recently, in the twentieth century, dominated in particular by the Stranger as Other and, in the context of the religious, the messianism of sects and evangelists. The same problematic appears, therefore, to envelop both philosophy and religious belief. When speaking in a factual manner about an 'end of belief' or a deconstruction of the structures of the Church, it also affects beliefs understood within the context of their institutional structures.

On the theoretical plane, Heidegger clearly made the transition from Idealism and current deconstructions of the theologico-religious possible, whether spontaneous or in a concerted manner. Passage, exit, end of philosophy, and so on – there is clearly a continuity of the problem. For idealism and post-Hegelian theologians, the issue concerns surpassing the common or ordinary consciousness that continues to subsist in philosophy in order better to recover this consciousness and lead it back towards its own essence, whereas the recent 'end' or 'gathering' (Heidegger) insists, less naïvely, upon an exit and proposes a return into essence, admitting that thought must gather itself before claiming to leave in a manner that is supposed different to Consciousness or Being. Even Marx participates, at the start at least, in this problematic of the exit and realization of philosophy – exit and realization are the inverse of one another. But Marx came to understand, little by little, what we now assume in a non-theology that starts from the identification of the Real and Man, understood as the content of the material base, namely the need to produce a new model and constitute organic force(s) through the force of the productive as much as the relation(s) of production, and, thereby, displace philosophy via a thought-science that Marx called 'historical materialism'.

But, perhaps, Marx does not reach the end or fulfilment of this Idea, still prematurely inscribing this in the material conditions of history and, in the end, giving way to a materialism suffused with philosophical prejudices. This is the general characteristic of the post-Marxist history of Marxism, the history of Christianity, and, finally, the history of philosophy. This epoch marks a liberal and religious regression, that is, a return to barely repressed or poorly analysed beliefs, giving rise to a return to fetishisms within a theologico-market or a generalized philosophico-market. When the problem has been posed in this way, with this 'half-will' that is the critique of the Church, Liberalism, and their excesses and failures, nothing is, then, more urgent than an 'exit' from the religious or philosophical Church and any supposed return (post-secular or post-theological) under a post-modern, sectarian, and multiple form. How could we be content with yet another, new critique of such 'indulgences' performed according to contemporary tastes as well as taboos? How could we be satisfied with a critique that fails to put into question the ensemble of first principles or axioms that structure Faith, God, Man, and Church? Let us state such a critique by transposing terms from Marxism into theology: the first organon of the proletariat or the first means of existence for the Faithful is a knowledge that must have the form of a universal non-theology and a theology transformed by faith solely on condition of *uniting faith and theology in faith alone*, forming thus a kind of a *thought-faith* and able, in this manner, to exit from an ideological and 'dominating' usage of the theologico-religious. Marx is as decisive for the faithful assumption of the theologico-religious as for the 'proletarian' assumption of the economy. This marks the first step towards establishing a 'first science' in relation to philosophy, called, respectively, for us a 'thought-faith' that uses theology only by completely denying any authority ascribed to it, but not, importantly, any usage. But such a step does not unify theology with philosophy or unify faith to belief in an exterior manner, like a transcendent ideological object or aim, and certainly avoids any implicit use of philosophical and theological categories. Philosophy and theology remain beliefs and ideologies of belief. But they are also reduced to the state of a contingent content that can be used as an organon in order to vanquish their state of ideology and belief.

The complexity and duplicity of theology will dissolve or lose their constitutive function, and the problem of a 'post-ecclesial exit' will no longer pose itself in terms of believers – both will vanish for the Faithful. If it is granted that faith is neither an event nor a formal or rational *a priori* belief but rather an *a priori* material *for* them, deduced, indeed, from Man-in-Person or made the vocation of the Faithful, then there will be no problem of leaving the theologico-religious or a return into the essence, especially when formulated with reference to the Church. There will be only the sufficiency of the theologico-religious itself such as employed and utilized by the machinery of churches, producing this impossible exit – creator of *resentiment* and bad consciousness.

From the exit from belief to faithful access

The 'exit' from the theologico-religious is spontaneously practised during the classical philosophical epoch of 'Construction' via the renewal of theologico-philosophical systems in the name of a better representation of the Real, understood as either Being or God. This is thematically practised in a voluntarist manner during the Greco-Judaic epoch of 'Deconstruction' in the name of the Real, understood this time as Other or Alterity. In both cases, despite the novelty of the second epoch, philosophy and theology conserve their traditional primacy; they both provide the horizon for the ultimate authority and legitimate or condemn certain practices of thought, controlling in every way the legitimate exercise of protest, contest, and revolt. If a new age for this problem is possible, then it must include the problem of an 'exit from the Church'. When this concerns only an exit from sects, however, then it must be regulated, as one has seen, by an *a priori* material – that is, via an *a priori* access to the theologico-philosophical. With respect to Man-in-Person, *a priori* access eliminates theological contortions of exit and return, on the one hand, and the sectarian twists and turns of leaving and coming back, on the other. The non-act of Man is *identically access and resistance to theo-logos*. In other words, the classical demand for an optimal representation, the linguistic turn, or even still Judaism and the history of persecution, along with other recent circumstances, like the bad consciousness of post-colonialism – both important for the Stranger and Alterity – are, here at least, not at all helpful to us, no more than the being-multiple of sects. Such instances are decisive for us only insofar as occasional material. The situation of struggle is clearly more complex for the Stranger-subject than for the Man-in-Person, who does not struggle but rather resists and accedes by fidelity, thereby making the *subjective* struggle that Man determines in-the-last instance possible. Every operation, like the 'deconstruction of Christianity', 'demytholgization' or even 'reformation' and 'liberation', must be founded upon a first, specifically human, resistance – fidelity. This explains why we have access to philosophy, without definitively ceding place to it through a simple constitutive recoil or retreat that would condemn this project to the vicious circle of philosophy. Man is no more constituted by Differ(e)ance than the Same; they hold good only for the Stranger-subject, who is affected by them like materials waiting to be transformed.

The problem of non-theology is resolved, first of all by fidelity, providing *a priori* access to the sphere of beliefs; then, upon this base, it can engage in a subjective struggle that marks a genuine *practical* exit from institutional theory and ecclesiology. On this material base of faith, the exit from theology towards what we have called its inferior level becomes a struggle or practice against contemplative theoreticism of the 'exit' or the arbitrary 'loss of faith'.

Towards a clandestine theology – Thought-faith

Religions are animated and worked up by the many causes of atheism. The most profound beliefs find their reasons for doubt on political, philosophical, and moral grounds. What matters to us here, however, is not the sceptical or anti-religious activities that accompany, clandestinely, all religions along the edge of its political borders. We make neither an history nor an archaeology. But it is certain, however, that the basis for any possible critique of God, religions, the Church, even faith itself has already been made, for example, during the sixteenth and seventeenth centuries, appearing often in literary form – sometimes openly, sometimes secretively. But we intend to seek another way than the route taken by a bellicose atheism, whose sole motivation would be the current restless trembling of a religious war emerging from hibernation and imposed by science and 'progress'. The problem will be precisely to know whether the quality and character of the clandestine must be used in an exterior manner, like writing against religion, or whether, on the contrary, this could not be the mode of an expression proper to an immanent atheism, faithful and militant, more exactly, a nontheism. From this non-theism, a religion or particular confession would constitute the model (in the sense of a concrete interpretation or an historical model for this militant posture). Our problem is to identify whether there is any such interpretation or model, that is, a particular religion, even confession, that might itself contain its own radical critique, even to the point of a renouncement-withoutnegation of God. This is an atheism that is immanent to religion, balancing itself with a militant ascesis that is also, paradoxically, clandestine in order to put the gods and the 'unique' and 'great' God back into a secondary position.

From this point of view, a criterion for radical atheism – radical, not absolute (see above) – can be found in Christianity, which will allow more easily for atheism or 'non-theism' through at least three impulses: (1) Christ Himself is, within the ecclesiological Christianity that suffocates Him at least, the first principal factor of the consequent non-theism, not summarily anti-religious for transcendent reasons but rather immanent or non-religious. Judaism could be another claimant but remains, however, content simply to eliminate the pagan gods, which are insufficiently transcendent, and Christ, too – the 'usurper messiah'. This phenomenon finds continued life in philosophy (Spinoza, Levinas, and the other tradition, Epicurus, Lucretius, Deleuze), while Christ renders the monotheist action of God – an action that He carries within Himself in an immanent manner – useless by evacuating the notion of 'creation'. (2) The second impulse is gnosis, which, for philosophical reasons or owing to Greek tolerance, spares the old Judaic God but, for more Christian reasons, only tolerates this God in order better to overpower the 'wickedness' and 'demented' character of the creator. (3) Finally, a third impulse comes from the Reformation, which pursues the general work of making God and His grace immanent, that is, making Him immediate – an action-without-church upon subjects. Each of these impulsions remains ambiguous with respect to the objectives that animate them and the means offered by them within a religious context, which present so many barriers or obstacles to the deployment of this non-theist or non-religious ascesis. The word of life of Christ, for example, gives rise to new philosophies, like the 'philosophy of Christianity' (Henry), which fail to achieve immanence but, instead, grant primacy to Life and the Living over the most radical Lived. Gnosis mixes Christ, the Jewish God, and the Greek mythological spirit together. Finally, the Reformation manifests some inconsistencies and assumes the risk of 'variations' but nevertheless fails to escape the clutches of philosophy and, instead, replaces the monolithic consistency of the Church with the consistency of philosophy, sometimes Hegelian, sometimes, Kierkegaardian, sometimes Heideggerian. In fact, the Reformation (and theology more broadly) does not know how to respond clearly, without ambiguity, to the question: *how to philosophise in or with*

Christ? Even if it posed the problem in the clearest possible terms. Beyond Christ, Christianity, under all forms, will not know how to put philosophy back in its place, which is not the primacy and site of the Real nor an anti-religious site for thought, but the non-religious – that is, in the Word. By making the religious immanent, the status of religion as the Real, along with the simple empirico-historical model, disappears. Christ alone is the subject who foresees His own consummation as God – that is, His death viewed as a religious entity. But this is not the Nietzschean death of the moral God, which is merely another way for religion to survive – the secret power of philosophy – but death upon the Cross. The Crucifixion grants the radically Lived primacy over life and death.

A definitively non-sufficient grace: Against creation

Man-in-Person and the *a priori* are the real, immanent content of God and His grace, which are both theologico-philosophical and transcendent symptoms. The *a priori* of faith is, here, grace, which gives the world, and, in giving this world, neither creates nor inhabits it. *A priori* faith or fidelity eliminates creation; it reveals the mythology of creation from whence all philosophical problems derive. There is no more a creation of the world than an exit from philosophy. Both *aporiae* are eliminated by means of an *a priori* access. Real fidelity is the substance, so-to-speak, of faith, and a principle of divine non-sufficiency. Saying 'God' instead of 'Man' is not a *lapsus*: God did not create the world nor what supposedly accompanied this creation, namely Good and Evil. But Man contains the reason to receive or refuse their primacy. The confusion of God with the world throughout 'creation' is the source of all amphibologies in theology and the phantasms that stalk them in the shadows. A certain Judaism sets us on the way: God 'does not have the means'; rather, He is precisely only the image of Man in the mirror of the world and believed, through an hallucination, to possess all the means to make the world, whereas He has no such means. Contrary to Christians who have wanted, at least partially, to replace messianism with grace, rejecting the Messiah in an undetermined future, we pose a double grace. On the one hand, grace is not insufficient but non-sufficient and the means for Man-in-Person to offer us the world and grant the means to transform it (since God did not create the world, we can and must transform it). On the other hand, grace is the subjective Coming, understood as the real clonage of the Messiah-subject, who comes before or in advance of the world this time as sufficient but changeable. If *a priori* grace gives us the world, without creating it, then the messianity of the subject, thus transformed, dedicates itself to the transformation of the world. We distinguish, then, two phases, both are in-the-last-humanity, that is, the being-given of the world in-the-last-instance. In the face of contemporary and post-ecclesial faith stands a 'half-belief' that remains nevertheless a belief, albeit, in part, without-Church. This is at once a non-religious faith and non-Jewish Coming or non-Christian hope. It will be necessary, therefore, to understand more rigorously the transformation of such terms through the function of Consummation, effectuated by the abandonment of creation.

The reformation as model for non-religion

The ultimate religious dimension is added to the empirico-transcendental structure of philosophy and penetrates every aspect, appearing in the middle of philosophy under (see above – the three 'ages') (1) the form of the 'gods of the cosmos' or linked to the cosmos,

(2) in Judaism, confusing itself with extreme transcendence, without any cosmic mediation between God and Man, and (3) in Catholic Christianity, the mediation of Christ, always transcendent, doubles itself by means of a cosmological mediation – that is, the world as the natural place of creatures and pagan philosophy as the organon or means of existence. Protestantism is the most Judaic of all Christian confessions. The Protestant reformation makes confession more radical and immanent through interiority, which remains a mode of transcendence, always one step away from real immanence. The mediation of Christ at once permits the passage from God to the World and the immediate essence of mediation, no longer through an exacerbated Judaic transcendence but an exacerbated interiority. Protestantism makes the mediation of Christ Jewish in terms of interiority. Luther is evidently still close to St Paul and the God of the Church on this point, where the greatest Lutheran invention stands: the principle of the sole efficacy of universal grace and the principle of universal *sacredoce*. But Münzer enriches the Reformation with a purer revolutionary aspect that could be called the principle of universal revolution. This minor branch of Protestantism has been, alas, forgotten – the lowly peasant. But we must search here for the most destructive power of revolt and the most decisive refusal of any compromise. The Reformation, like everything else, must pass through a number of phases that can be formulated in the following manner. There is, first of all, Luther, eruptive and precipitative, yet incomplete, short-lived, and inevitably seeking help and assistance from princes, that is, the authority of Authority. There is, second, the Münzerian repetition of the Lutheran Reformation, which stands as a second, greater emergence, but nevertheless attached, in the end, to the vicious circle of Authority. In the end, there is the completely subjective and Calvinist formulation of the action of the subject upon and within the world. Put another way: (1) the Lutheran emergence

of the grace that saves us and assumes primacy is the principle, more than simply first, that is, the principle posing primacy in the first place – the chief invention of Luther – but nevertheless as an undetermined or intra-worldly liberation; there is (2) the Münzerian principle of the revolutionary subject, that is, the *a priori* struggle against all power and the force of resistance to all political authority form a single body, from our point of view, with the principle of universal *sacredoce*; there is, in the end, (3) the Calvinist principle that poses the institution or their relation to the world along with the problem of two powers, that is, the duality of struggle and obedience and the double decision. This simple formalization of the Reformation distinguishes the principles underpinning it from their historical bedrock and recognizes their own universality at the very limits of the universality of philosophy and even founded, in part, outside of it. The principles underpinning the Reformation prepare the way for a more radical non-religion, non-history and non-theology, as symptoms for the subject. This formalism is, however, no longer rationalist – that is, a Kantian rationalization of the 'Lutheran' affect. Only the *a priori* and transcendental that is deduced from Man *alone* can be equal to the world-form – it is not at all the substance that fills the world. Such a perspective allows for the passage beyond Lutheranism as well as Kant and Fichte. The Reformation, as historico-religious phenomenon, is far from being the sole material for non-theology, even if it is a very personal symptom, but certainly models an interpretation that is particularly close to the formalization put forward – a possible modelization of non-religion.

The consummation of time

It is now possible to offer a first approximation of three distinct ages or styles of philosophy:

(1) the classical logocentric Construction (upon bases, foundations, axioms, and principles);

(2) the Greco-Judaic, post-modern Deconstruction (by alterity); and

(3) the non-philosophical Consummation or Christo-fiction (by fidelity and messianity)

On the basis of an 'exit' from belief and the Church in general, that is, exit as *a priori* access, what does the transformation of the theologico-religious world concretely mean, if not its consummation as a mixture of philosophy and beliefs? How should we understand this Consummation? Could it be the real node for the 'transformation of the world' that Marx and Feuerbach called for?

Religion has primacy over philosophy. This thesis is, doubtless, full of exceptions and open to interpretation. But in order to justify this claim, we pose a global architecture of science as base, philosophy as organon, and religion as the primacy of the Real, crowning the edifice. From the perspective of clandestine theology, what, on the one hand, is the specificity of Christianity with respect to other religions and, on the other, the effect of Christ on the autonomy of philosophy, received from the Greeks? We have interpreted Christianity, when taken back to the person and teachings of Christ, first of all, as a radical inversion of the relation between faith and religion, then as an immanent becoming of mediation, and, finally, now as the consummation of religion. Together they form the 'system': the primacy of Man-in-Person, the primacy of faith over religious belief or the priority of the Other as Stranger-subject, where mediation remains immanent, and, finally, the consummation of the theologico-religious form of the world by subjects. Christianity as an historico-religious formation is evidently only a symptom of this inversion of faith and religion, that is, this becoming immanent of faith, independent from beliefs.

In this last possible religious context, Christianity only makes faith immanent in a particular reality, rather than a radical immanence.

The consummation of the death and sacrifice of Christ can be conveyed or brought to the world. It is the world that is now consummated. This 'conveyance' is key. The sacrifice of Christ means that 'all is consummated'. But this total consummation implicates the world that is sacrificed by the Christic Coming. This marks the very idea of an 'end of philosophical or theological time' that is not, importantly, an autonomous end, like a philosophical re-affirmation of itself, but one that is at once heteronomous and immanent. It is a pure Coming without 'anything' that might come, only the unfolding of immanence; in other words, a Coming that would not or will not have been pre-destined or awaited. Neither Greek desire nor Jewish anticipation nor Christian hope can consummate the Whole of history and the world. Philosophical desire believes itself to be the Whole or All and what makes world, Jewish messianic anticipation resolves the Whole into a pure materiality, and Christian hope turns the All into a return understood as a repetition of history. But the radical consummation of the Whole can be done by the Stranger-subject alone. The three relations to the world are, in the end, set within a theologico-religious horizon that each then cuts up and distributes at the risk of an interminable repetition. The death of Christ is too often understood solely in the narrow and restricted sense of an accomplishment or fulfilment of His life, mission, and sacrifice. But how would death explain that whoever saw Him saw the Father? The consummation of the world-form, understood successively as hallucinatory (for Man) then as illusory (for the subject), is the same thing leaving itself in the mid- or half-leap backwards of the subject. Here, the practical exit from philosophy and its subsequent transformation or consummation designates the same phenomenon.

Retreat and grace

Let us recapitulate one last time the distinction between a philosophico-religious theology and a generic or 'clandestine' theology by appealing to the Judaic solution for our guiding example. A modality of Judaism, namely the Kabbalah, attributes creation to the withdrawal or retreat of God, who freely limits His Being-All in order to give way for the time and space of man. Like any retreat, it is a 'backward' or 'reverse' operation of transcendence – that is, the All affecting itself by weakness and lack. This configuration remains inscribed in the broadest and most insistent invariants of philosophy, namely the primacy of the Whole or All as the bearer of authority, the first or originary operation of 'differe(a)nce of the origin', and so on. This is clearly not a classical ontology of *causa sui* or auto-production (Spinoza, Nietzsche, Deleuze) but rather another, tragic tradition that is almost like the reverse of the classical one. The tragic tradition draws its 'Western' credentials from Greek tragedy – for example, Hölderlin's 'categorical deviation' or the Kantian liberation of space and time that results from the retreat – with the intermediary stage finding its expression in the tragic vision of the *Deus absconditus* that sets the physical world loose (Pascal and Kant), and, finally, the contemporary accomplishment of this vision in deconstruction, where the Logos affects or hetero-affects itself via a retreat, withdrawal, or an active difference. There is, then, an ensemble of distinctive traits that mark the tragic tradition and forms a network of relations that appear anew in contemporary thought, Levinas and Derrida included. This network revolves around Greek tragedy and the Kabbalah, each sharing the common affirmation of an hyperbolic transcendence of an infinite and celestial being that betokens the finite liberty and responsibility of man that is tolerated or imposed upon him by God's retreat. There are a few differences and nuances between the two that are not negligible: the Sophoclean deviation from God with respect to man (e.g. Oedipus) differs from the Kabbalah's description of God's retreat into Himself, granting via this contraction the relative autonomy of man. This sobering and tragic figure that the absence of God bequeaths to man is precisely what condemns him to an immemorial errancy or interminable work.

The consummation of the God-world holds as much for the mysticism of the retreat, the Greco-philosophical tragic tradition, as well as the Greco-Judaic deconstruction, without speaking about the ideology of absence or lack that psychoanalysis sets at the very heart of the Real and the subject. Man-in-Person is hardly visible and scarcely hidden, unfolding like a coming or grace that reveals the world as the philosophico-religious world. A minimal yet radical nuance distinguishes the retreat of God before Man and the subtraction of Man from God: the retreat is an operation that supposes that the Whole or All is real and that transcendence is law, while subtraction (even 'without-subtraction') supposes that Man is real and immanence is the law of liberty. Man is not withdrawn from himself and does not begin with self-sacrifice or auto-mutilation. The retreat leaves the 'bad positivity' of the Whole or All to subsist beneath what remains and does not gain the 'good positivity' of immanence. Philosophy leaves the subject to shoulder the burden of the divine retreat or to repose in some way within this withdrawal; it is the *volte-face* of the subject or man that keeps hold of the divine retreat, so that everything passes between man and God in accordance with the onto-theo-logical axis. By contrast, the generic signifies that Man subtracts via primacy, not priority, even if this primacy is deployed in order to produce a priority that is subtracted *a priori* from the world. *God withdraws, while Man resists and consummates the world.* God withdraws before the world. But this is a negative conception that supposes the initial positivity of the world, which can be seen, for example, in deconstruction. Man, however, resists and transforms (or consummates) the world. Both indicate very different creative goods and bounties.

Why? Beyond the perpetual problem of Christian theology, namely the consummation of the Law that has been reduced (or not) to a dialectical overcoming, lies the more profound problem concerning the relation between God and Man in terms of struggle. In the pre-Christian, tragic, Kabbalist, deconstructionist context, obsessed with the responsibility for God or the Other, primacy is understood as a problem of struggle and conflict – or even worse the form of a struggle for vital space. This is the old mythological confusion of Man and subject that supposes their reversibility. But, above all, this tragico-Judaic conception is founded upon a first struggle for the vital space and time of existence. Space and time are the stakes of the struggle between God and Man, who share a common and global space-time. The economy of religion is an economy of scarcity that annuls the non-economy of grace. This struggle for primacy that the Whole or All arrogates to itself according to more tenacious and archaic pagan prejudices founds itself upon a principle of equivalence that distributes the terms. The Jews and 'we-the-philosophers' have set scarcity, struggle, and conflict in the Heavens. But Christianity brings the possibility of grace, that is, the principle of the radical gift that is proper to Man, understood as the messianity at the foundation of the Stranger-subject. The real core of eternity is the non-temporal coming, *without* scarcity, that distributes itself for the world. Man-in-Person is Stranger to the Whole or All of the infinite space-time, which is always and already given or anticipated in some way and confused with God, a divine retreat, or even a categorical deviation (see above). The yoke of the Whole or All was cast off in philosophy by Kant and then Heidegger via the insertion of an *a priori* between the subject and a metaphysics that is irreducible to man. But both still attach this *a priori* to space-time and assign this to the subject, not to Man. There is nothing in common between Man and the world, including the God-world. There is no law superior to Man that would oblige him to withdraw or distribute himself in some way throughout the world. The expansion of the biological, cultural, religious, and economic forms of existence is inevitable in the order of the world and possesses a certain degree of legitimacy, or at the very least necessity. But this expansion carries much less legitimacy, perhaps none at all after the advent of Christianity, when it is made ideologically vital and spiritual, reflecting the struggle for space and time in Man and the subject. How could a God withdraw from this struggle in creation, without being animated in some way by jealousy and malice? The transformation of the world is not a vital expansion, like the perverse effect of a retreat; on the contrary, it is a pre- or ante-spatiotemporal flux of grace. Christianity signifies the new primacy of grace over the retreat or withdrawal of the divine, privileging the peace between God and man. But this is, importantly, a non-contractual peace and, above all, not an 'alliance' or 'covenant', even a 'new covenant'. It signals, in the end, a transformation of war into the struggle with the world alone, that is, a consummation of a war that is identical with the world. Understood as a simple model for interpretation or a modelling of non-theology, the simplicity of grace puts an end to the naturally perverse logic of philosophy such as it has been adopted and reinforced by the maliciousness of the Jewish God and the greatest monotheistic God.

We could ask, more broadly, whether any and every monotheistic God does not have a vocation for the ontological malignity of omnipotence, like the Jewish God? How could such a God survive creation as well as the ever necessary retreat or withdrawal from it, if not by an hegemonic expansion and accumulation of 'capital' in the form of supposed properties, attributes, effects, and miracles? God is the paradigm of survival for us: the Great Survivor, imprinting His mark upon all 'victims' that serves to define them. Man is not created in the image of God – the victim is made in His image. Classical ontology, namely that of perfections and hyperbolic substantiality, avoids the retreat or withdrawal, but only in a superficial way; it is condemned to make excuses for itself via theodicies that rest upon mere philosophical quibbles and pitiable subtleties. Having never operated an originary retreat, classical ontology is condemned to draw back and look out from the perspective of creation alone, which is another possible end to this human–divine war. As the most powerful phantasm of theology and philosophy, creation must be renounced. This phantasm depends upon an artful transformation, the passive reception of a mechanical effect, a filiation, a model, an imprint, an image, and so on and so forth. In every case, creation is a vicious circle. It can anticipate itself through a duplication, conceptual doubling, and/or missing itself, in some way, through delay, stutter, deconstruction; it can even fail completely, owing to an excess of ambition – something the gnostics denounce. Either creation forms an identity that is transcendent, that is, an act *and* the product of this act, an identity of producer and product, as some Jewish scholars have posed, like a filiation, or it forms an act of descent that resolves the *aporia* through materialism, whereby the effects of creation are set within the material order – matter being always a limit phenomena of reception and held firm by a transcendent act. Man is the living rejection of creation, either as a withdrawal or as a positive act – that is, as a self-anticipating, duplicative, or vicious act. Only an immanent practice of transformation or even – the latter still supposing matter as a receptacle – a practice of radical consummation of the material or materiality that constitutes the world-form can avoid the *aporiae* of creation. It is better to recognize here an occasional 'pre-donation' of the world, like a material awaiting consummation, without appealing to creation, and presume an *a priori* organon as the relatively autonomous means for this consumption of existence that is identical in-last-instance to Man.

The subversion of responsibility, in the Judaic sense, leads in the end to the discovery of the Jewish struggle *with* God (and not '*against*' Him). But the weakness of absolute evil cannot bring about a passage to the stage of radical evil. Doubtless, the messianism of responsibility makes clear that this war between man and God arises from a religious link between man and the Other. But religion is not the sole witness to this conflict. The real content of responsibility-for-the-Other-Man is the ultimate responsibility for the struggle waged between Man and God. The fact that 'space-time' either precedes their relation or even results from this conflict indicates the firm hold space-time has over them. Opposite this we will pose grace or clonage, wherein they are effectuated. There is, on one side, the infinite space through which God or a duplicitous transcendent agent acts *against* Man or keeps him in a subordinate position, and, on the other side, grace as the action of Man passing through the time and the space of the world, like an invariant.

At the very moment when every kind of struggle, conflict, and war multiplies, increasing their intolerable psychological burden, we dare to announce, without shame or any sense of ridicule, the messianity of an age of grace. Where is peace, if not in we-the-humans, partially outside or extra to the subject, like a new organon? The confusion often made that we must strive to undo concerns not only the mixing of Man-in-Person and the subject but also the muddling of radical peace, which is a true means for ethical and faithful existence, and worldly peace, understood as the stability that precedes or awaits war. An *a priori* peace is the immediate organon of immanence-in-person, that is, the act of human non-action. This is, perhaps, the greatest invention of Christianity, even if this has not yet been adequately conceptualized. We will pose two theorems: (1) peace is not an Ideal placed before and beneath us, simply to be hoped for or realized 'in the world'. Peace does not have to-be-in-the-world, only *for* the world; it is an *a priori* organon for the consummation of the theologico-religious struggle in the world. The peace-instrument and the mixtures of war-and-peace that form their usual concept can be distinguished by a unilateral duality. (2) Peace is utopian by virtue of being-human and to the extent that being material and empty of any historical or apocalyptic content; the immanence of this utopia excludes the apocalypse, although it may admit this but only as an occasion.

From sin to evil

It is possible, perhaps, to identify a religion without sin, but difficult, near impossible, to imagine one without evil. Sin is a category that is far too Christian to be easily transferable to another religion; it is too personal and subjective to be worth anything outside creation. By contrast, evil is much more universal and anonymous, more mythological, too. But if evil is not co-extensive with sin, then it has a less authentically Christian sense. Indeed, sin retroactively receives sense and meaning from the salvation assumed by Christ. Understood as 'original', sin is made immanent by Christianity. But such interwoven exchanges do not directly concern us here. Within the religious horizon of philosophy, defined strictly as a transcendental device, can be found the most anonymous transcendentals, like Good and Evil, which are supposed to be universal and applicable or predicable to each and every being. In virtue of their convertible nature, transcendentals, like the Good, only have meaning as the ultimate or theological closure of the philosophical circle. The onto-theological circle is, for the faithful, precisely the model for and concentration of a much deeper Evil. Such an Evil can only be identified by the faithful as precisely what tends to capture and destroy the messianity of faith by entering into a struggle against it. The operation of the faithful subject is quite complex: Good and Evil, like great shadows keeping Man company, pass through many (philosophical) circles that ultimately secure the precarious primacy of the Good. Insofar as messianic, the subject has always decided, without any arbitrary will, that the Good is diminished by the action of Evil through its anti-human anonymity. Both form a hallucinatory and deceptive doublet. This decision determines the identity of Evil in the sense that this decision is not *made by* the subject nor *decides* the subject but precisely decides, that is, determines, the subject's discourse about them. Through a certain righteousness or rectitude, the subject does not recognize itself in this perverse play; rather, the subject is affirmed in a clandestine manner as Man-in-Person, who asserts primacy over the Good itself, which the subject finds too absolute *not* to be relative, too excessive *not* to betray him or her. Man is foreclosed to the Good as much as Evil. Rejecting the sin(s) that overwhelm 'him' through their religious association, Man places subjective evil in its proper place, namely the world. This gesture of rejection is not, however, a simple reversal that would make evil appear as simply what insists on the other side of the Good; rather, such a rejection decides what the subject already understood or suspected at the very depths of Evil. What is the significance of the claim that the world, understood as the onto-theological Logos, is the form of Evil, that is, Evil-in-Person? We stand close to a gnostic affect, namely an apparent 'psychologization' and 'mythologization' of Evil, but for completely difference reasons, which, being human through and through, means that this is no longer psychological (or mythological), but rather mathematical. This retains the Christian power to make Evil immanent, thereby excluding the mythological as well as any external transcendence, but also concentrates this where religion and gnosis situate it, namely the World. What must be understood now is the significance of this concentration of Universal Evil in the World (insofar as the world is, indeed, universal in accordance with its own logic). Man insofar as the bearer of the title 'in-Person' is torn from – that is, in fact, to suggest given to – the Trinity, which has until now divided and dispersed him, and clones the faithful subject, who decides Evil is inherent to the self (as found in the World), like being 'riveted' (Levinas), even doubly riveted, doubly bound to itself. The world is not necessarily and eternally Evil. This is still precisely a religious thesis of gnosis; it is a place or occasion, Evil acting as the double bondage of the subject or an over-alienation, that is, an over-identification of the Stranger – the alienation of the Stranger can only be an hallucinatory identification. More than ever, Evil is a condition, more strictly subjective than human; it could even be understood as a situation that limits destruction to the salvation of the subject-in-the-world. Christianity made Evil into a 'bad' universalization, placing Man under this condition, while it is only a subjective situation. Christianity made Evil coextensive with the plane of salvation, which is meant to end with a regeneration of men as sinners. If Man-in-Person is foreclosed to sin, and therefore open in an *a priori* manner insofar as a Messianic Outside, if Man, furthermore, decides rather on the extension and depth of Evil, not religion, then Man is for eternity the Saviour-without-salvation, placing Evil within the human condition. There is no historical plan for salvation. There is precisely only a human *a priori* for salvation that extends down towards the very foundations of the World. This restriction to the situation of the subject thus set under the condition of the human allows for the gathering together of Evil understood now as the *narcissism* of the world. This narcissism remains nonetheless decided for all eternity, rather than substantial; it is decided, and so already elevated, immanently, by the subject, that is, identified as hallucinatory and illusory. Over-alienation or over-identification can only affect the subject as the duplicity of being-riveted to oneself. But being-riveted is an hallucination, *then* an illusion; it is the way in which over-alienation is real. Salvation has already come to or, more precisely, sub-tended, clandestinely, the World. The subject, assuming messianity in a clandestine manner, releases itself from this confusion between the World and Man, and causes the World to come into the place assigned to it by Man. The subject is indebted to Man. When the subject imagines itself to be in the world, only then does it receive its share of evil – it is the entirety of philosophy and religion put together.

A clandestine and messianic life

Christology turned the greater part of philosophy towards the theme of a more individual and immanent life than the contemplative life of the Greek sage. Even God has become more living or alive with Christ. This is especially true in recent phenomenologies and philosophies of life, where the meaning of the immanent life of God has been sharply and radically elucidated on the basis of 'auto-affection' (Henry). This great transcendental conquest is accomplished in the spirit of a Christocentrism that undertakes a critique of the Greek ontological presuppositions that pose the primacy of transcendence (over immanence) and stands in *de facto* opposition to ontologies of the supposed immanence of the 'life-world' (Husserl). While retaining this invention of the radical immanence of human life, according to the Christian context, we will make several modifications to this life now made immanent. (1) Christianity is no longer a context, that is, a religious environment for non-Christianity; it is rather a symptom, a material, and, in the end, a possible model. Christocentrism is precisely for this reason excluded completely, whilst at the same time condensed into what non-Christianity makes of and owes to it. (2) Christ cannot be an 'archi-transcendental Son (Henry)', who would return once again to the Father in a final gesture of transcendence – the Father as the 'sub-life' of the Son. On the contrary, the Son is entirely the last instance of Man-in-Person, adding the messianity of Man to the (human) subject, without adding, ascribing, or removing anything from Man in this discourse. The Father is definitively annihilated or returned to the presuppositions that make up the fabric of the world. As Man-in-Person, the subject-messiah gathers together and condenses every Real possible, even if the messianic acts of this subject can be understood to be determined in last-instance by Man. (3) The Last Instance signifies that the Real is given in a radical way along with the subject such that it 'adds' to the subject only a relation to the world. This final instance has nothing to do with transcendence, whether this be understood as the transcendence of God or a kind of 'transcendence in immanence' understood along the lines of Christocentrism. On the contrary, the Last Instance delivers us from the religious and philosophical worlds. We reject the formula 'who has seen the Son has also seen the Father' along with the reciprocal relation (Son-Father). Only the first term is 'revolutionary' and forbids the return of religion in the Messiah. There is no convertibility or reversibility between Father and Son, except for nostalgia, guilt, and love, which do not form an 'ontology' with a rigorous axiomatic. The supposed reversibility between the two terms is a Greco-philosophical theorem as well as an axiom that forms the basis for the fundamental confusion found in the dogmas of Christianity and, for this reason, are much deeper than the 'intuitive' presuppositions that Henry detects and criticizes in philosophy. This reciprocal relation has not been demonstrated and could only rest upon axioms that are not counted among them. This is the reason Christianity is only a transcendent model – indeed, rigorously indemonstrable – for axioms like 'He who has seen the Son in Man does not have the desire to see the Father, and, indeed, sees nothing of the Father, but sees, instead, the world in the Son – the world that the Son acts'. (4) The Son is, indeed, a transcendental subject, but only real in-the-last-instance. This means that the Father cannot be concluded from the Son, drawing us back to revelation, like an ascent, as opposed to Judaism, which makes revelation a 'decent' and a filiation or creation. The Last Instance is no more a descent than an ascent, no more a procession than a conversion; it is a coming that draws meaning only from the 'sub-tending' or clandestine character of Man – the giver of the World – and takes its meaning only as the 'sub-arrival' or the clandestine character of the Giver, Man of the World. This 'sub-tending' is assumed in a Messianic operation for the World and is entirely the work of the subject. (5) Transcendental auto-affection at best places the archi-living of Christ at the 'centre' – understood in a phenomenological manner – and can only model an immanence that is too invisible to be considered auto-affective. Like any transcendental device, the phenomenological Christ differentiates in the same gesture the world that it abandons and the celestial kingdom of the Father. The philosophical transcendental, even before any Christian interpretation, is the sword that divides people and cuts into life. The philosophico-phenomenological tradition gives an overly reifying and naïve interpretation of the transcendental subject found at work in Kantian/post-Kantian philosophy and phenomenology. Both unduly favour the unity of the subject and consciousness as apperception. The transcendental is the machine for philosophical war *par excellence*. When the transcendental is put under a real condition, then more than a unilateral duality, without division, is introduced, at once more supple and more radical, standing between two statutes of the 'same' world – the one insofar as sufficient, the other insofar as transfigured in the messianic vision. 'Christ with the sword' is a formula that admits at least two heterogeneous meanings. (6) The time of salvation does not completely destroy Greek temporality. But this does not undermine the claim that the latter is circular. Rather, the former preserves a final circularity in several respects, despite the flattening of soteriological time, gradation (or emanation), and infinite opening. This temporality returns Christ, too – that is, the imminence of time, the last judgement, and, in the end, 'life' itself or the 'living' announced in the Gospels that remain inseparable from the Greek closure of time and eternity, according to which life will always be an image. The structure of the horizon is usually philosophical and insinuates itself into the fabric of Christianity, with or without a reverse or inverse side. This structure is not 'horizontal' in the ordinary sense but always vertical at the same time as flat; it is a diagonal or a transversal that results from the coordination of two philosophical forces (*meta-* and *epekeina-*). When the radical immanence of the Real 'sub-tends' as a certain 'thrown-without-throwness' that Man *a priori* 'sends' over the world, like a unilateral pulsion that the subject assumes and directs locally upon an occasion, or a symptom of the world (upon the onto-theological understood as the form of the world), then the structure of the horizon finds itself really abandoned, along with any 'semi-verticality' or inclination of the plane. There is no horizontal or vertical, and no philosophical flatness in the operation of salvation. (7) Finally, and more profoundly still, the horizon is at best understood and then refused insofar as finitude by some contemporary philosophers (e.g. Henry, in the name of the infinity of life, and Badiou, in the name of the mathematical infinity of being). In both cases, however, there is the question regarding what the infinite exactly owes to a finitude that is specific to it, that is, no longer set within the Greek horizon of finitude – that both Henry and Badiou criticize – but rather within a finitude of being-created that is linked to an auto-affection that is still transcendental (Henry) and a finiteness of the set-theoretical form needed to contain the mathematical infinity of the 'multiple of multiples' or the void (Badiou). The extrinsic finitude of the created-being limits the infinite-without-horizon. Creation has thus replaced the Greco-cosmic horizon. The set-theoretical form that allows for the axiomatic exploitation of mathematics limits the infinity of the multiple that is indebted to being, understood as a presentation. The announced exclusion of any unity via transcendence or the 'count-as-one' of the calculus allows for the preservation of their hidden yet constitutive form or double, that is, a final transcendence of the transcendental that will find itself revealed like the transcendence of God, in terms of either Life (Henry) or the final transcendence of the Whole, understood as the anti-numerical form of the multiple (Badiou). This is the last consistency that makes possible an immanent or unreflected knowledge of the infinite transcendental *ego* or of mathematics. The conclusion taken from this will be that philosophy has never really questioned the secret call to a presupposed 'Radical Identity' that lies deep within the philosophical binding together of the two dimensions that comprise the horizon (seen in Henry and Badiou) and that can only be announced in this context in the form of a supplement to transcendence. Nothing philosophical that makes use of phenomenologico-Christian or mathematico-materialistic operations can therefore pose a radical infinite, only an absolute infinite that is secretly finite – limited by the extent of its own transcendence. By all accounts this makes for an infinite openness for as long as this is solicited within the context of a philosophy that cannot be free of any finitude or closure – a 'Greek' destiny – even the closure of infinity. It does not and cannot help sinking into itself, taking pleasure in itself or returning to what the infinite has always been – an infinite self-concealment up to the gap or fissure in itself, the infinite form of the auto-position.

The infinite is a 'concept-trap' that seems to be autonomous, especially if understood as absolute. But nothing absolute can do without finitude or a form that is raised and erased, like the unfolding of a dialectic. We call radical infinity an infinity of immanence, that is, intrinsically finite, without form, whether internal or external.

The task of thinking the infinite remains, therefore, beyond philosophy; it is in reality, and by every philosophical account, a non-philosophical task and, perhaps, even a non-task, that is, a non-problem and an answer without question, whereby the question would serve only to limit the infinite and turn this into a symptom under the pretext of welcoming it, pushing the infinite into conformity with already established standards. What should now be clear is that it is a religious response that awaits us as much as a philosophical one. But with this key difference: this time the answer is impossible for philosophical questions – it is an unexpected answer and, in every way, inadmissible as much as irrefutable. Either the infinite is pre-formed philosophically, for example, via a mathematical form or a transcendent God or the infinite comes, 'sub-tends' in a wholly clandestine manner, offering a light proper to the secret, and no longer dissimulated or distorted in the gloomy half-light of mystery. The most unexpected and the most unhoped-for infinite comes neither from afar, from above, from the horizon, nor the inverse or reverse of this horizon, but from the most invisible aspect or part of ourselves, we, who are beings of infinite immanence, like God, is a being of infinite transcendence. In the beginning there is neither Word nor Action, only Mirage – the reflection of Man in the world, a gigantic and distorted reflection.

Notes

Translator's note

1 See Quentin Meillassoux, *After Finitude*, trans. by Ray Brassier (London: Continuum, 2009), Ch 2 for a definition of 'weak' and 'strong' correlationism in contemporary thought.
2 Ó Maoilearca, *All Thoughts Are Equal: Laruelle and Non-Human Philosophy* (Minneapolis: University of Minnesota Press, 2015), p. 8.
3 Laruelle, *Philosophy and Non-Philosophy*, trans. by Anthony Paul Smith (London: Bloomsbury, 2017), p. 42.
4 Marjorie Gracieuse, 'Laruelle Facing Deleuze' in *Laruelle and Non-Philosophy*, ed by John Mullarkey and Anthony Paul Smith (Edinburgh: Edinburgh University Press, 2012), p. 51.
5 While few openly endorsed the name 'speculative realism', at least initially, it has nevertheless gained currency in philosophical circles over the past decade. There are many figures in this Anglo-American and French constellation of twenty-first-century thought, some of the most well-known figures include Ray Brassier, Graham Harman, and Timothy Morton as well as Quentin Meillassoux.
6 See Graham Harman's review of Laruelle's *Philosophies of Difference: A Critical Introduction to Non-Philosophy* in Notre Dame Philosophical Reviews (2011).
7 Some of Laruelle's early works focus on Nietzsche and Heidegger (for example, *Nietzsche contre Heidegger* [1977] and *Le Déclin de l'écriture* [1977]), while his *Philosophies of Difference* (1986 [French]; 2010 [English]) engages directly with Hegel, Nietzsche-Deleuze, Heidegger, and Derrida.
8 Gilles Deleuze, *Difference and Repetition*, trans. by Paul Patton (London: Continuum, 2004), p. 36.
9 See François Laruelle, *Introduction au non-marxisme* (Paris: PUF, 2000), pp. 46–7, for a brief description of clonage and the clone.

10 Clandestine Theology, p. 12.
11 Ibid., p. 4.
12 Ibid., p. 5.
13 Ibid., p. 78.
14 Ibid., p. 77.
15 For a discussion of the relation between non-philosophy and humanism, post-humanism and the idea of the non-human, see Ò Maoilearca, 'The Animal Line' and Ian James, 'The Nonhuman Demand' in *Paragraph*, vol 42, no 1 (2019).
16 Clandestine Theology, p. 29.
17 See Edmund Husserl, Husserl, *Ideas Pertaining to a Pure Phenomenology and to a Phenomenological Philosophy*, trans. by F. Kersten (The Hague: Martinus Nijhoff, 1982), §124.
18 This forms a trilogy of works: Henry, *Incarnation: A Philosophy of the Flesh*, trans. by Karl Hefty (Evanston: Northwestern University Press, 2015); *I Am, the Truth: Toward a Philosophy of Christianity*, trans. by Susan Emmanuel (Stanford: Stanford University Press, 2002); *Words of Christ*, trans. by Christina M. Gschwandtner (Cambridge: Wm. B. Eerdmans, 2012).
19 See Michel Henry, *Material Phenomenology*, trans. by Scott Davidson (New York: Fordham University Press, 2008).
20 See Henry, *Words of Christ*, trans. by Christina Gschwandtner (Michigan: Eerdmans Publishing Company, 2011).
21 François Laruelle, *Introduction au non-marxisme*, p. 41 (my own translation)
22 See Henry, *I Am the Truth*, trans. by Susan Emanuel (Stanford: Stanford University Press, 2002).
23 Clandestine Theology, p. 68.
24 Ibid., p. 62.
25 Ibid., p. 52.
26 Ibid., p. 67.
27 Ibid., p. 63.
28 Ibid., p. 64.
29 Ibid., p. 84.
30 Ibid., p. 94.
31 Ibid., p. 123.
32 Ibid., p. 130.
33 Ibid.
34 Ibid., p. 123.
35 Ibid., p. 102.
36 See Ibid., p. 48.
37 Ibid., p. 107.

38 Ibid., p. 104.
39 Ibid.
40 Ibid., p. 123.
41 Katerina Kolozova, *Toward a Radical Metaphysics of Socialism, Marx and Laruelle* (New York: Punctum, 2015), p. 37.
42 Ibid.
43 Ray Brassier, *Nihil Unbound: Enlightenment and Extinction* (London: Palgrave Macmillan, 2007), p. 137.
44 François Laruelle, *Théorie des Étrangers* (Paris: Éditions Kimé, 1998), p. 24.
45 John Ò Maoilearca, 'The Animal Line, On the Possibility of a "Laruellean" Non-Human Philosophy' in *Angelaki: Journal of the Theoretical Humanities*, vol 19, no 2 (June 2014).
46 Clandestine Theology, p. 131.
47 Falque, *Dieu, la chair, et l'autre, D'Irénée à Duns Scot* (Paris: PUF, 2008), p. 31.
48 Pierre Hadot, *Exercices spirituels et philosophie antique* (Paris: Études augustiniennes, 1981), p. 56.
49 Cf. Falque, *Dieu, la chair, et l'autre*, pp. 31–2.
50 Stanislas Breton, *Le Verbe et la croix* (Paris: Mame-Desclée, 2010) Ch 3, pp. 53–75.
51 Ibid., p. 52.
52 Clandestine Theology, p. 46.
53 Ibid., p. 79.
54 Breton, *op. cit.*, p. 44.

Chapter 2

1 Alain Badiou, *Saint St Paul: The Foundation of Universalism* (Stanford: Stanford University Press, 2003), p. 48.
2 Ibid., pp. 48–9.
3 Ibid., p. 54.

Index

Badiou, Alain 1–5, 8, 65–7, 78–9, 83, 88, 130, 180–1

Deleuze, Gilles 79, 85, 89, 119, 123, 130, 161

Derrida, Jacques 100, 135, 168
and Christianity 85–6, 105, 141, 159
deconstruction 2, 39, 43, 82, 84, 107, 108, 144–5, 153, 155, 158, 165, 166, 168–70, 172
Evil 90–1, 134, 150–3, 162, 173, 174–7

Feuerbach, Ludwig Andreas von 11–13, 19, 28, 52, 114, 166, 172

grace 22, 23–5, 29, 38, 45–6, 154, 161, 162–5, 169–71, 173

Hegel, Georg Wilhelm Friedrich 25, 26, 32, 62, 65, 68, 78, 82, 83, 133, 147
Hegelianism 11, 16, 52, 114, 144, 161

Heidegger, Martin 23, 83, 129, 141, 143, 155–6, 161, 170

Henry, Michel 55, 57–8, 62, 68, 114, 161, 177, 178, 180–1, 184

Holy Spirit 96–7, 131–2

Jesus 38, 40, 49, 54–8, 68–72, 74, 92, 94, 95, 122

Kant, Immanuel 100, 165, 168, 170
Kantian 151, 165, 168, 179
post-Kantian 82, 179

Kierkegaard, Søren 13, 21, 26, 114, 154, 161

Levinas, Emmanuel 3, 21, 79, 143, 154, 161, 168
and Evil 91, 152, 176

Marion, Jean-Luc 21, 143

Reformation 81, 109, 110, 112, 159, 161, 164–5
Calvin, John 164–5
Luther, Martin 76, 109, 164–5
Münzer, Thomas 164–5
Veron, Fr François 110–11
Vögelin, Ernst 83
Resurrection 45, 54–6, 62–7, 69, 71, 72, 78, 87–8, 93, 94, 96, 100, 116 *see also* St Paul

St Paul 60, 74, 75–9, 80, 95, 113, 122, 164
and the Resurrection 54–6, 62, 65–72, 88, 92–3, 116

Trinity 1–3, 96, 121, 127, 128, 130–6, 139, 176

www.ingramcontent.com/pod-product-compliance
Lightning Source LLC
Chambersburg PA
CBHW060950230426
43665CB00015B/2140